At Issue

The United Nations

Other books in the At Issue series:

Alcohol Abuse

Book Banning

Bulimia

Can Diets Be Harmful?

Child Athletes

Date Rape

Does Capital Punishment Deter Crime?

Drunk Driving

Extreme Sports

Homeschooling

Human Embryo Experimentation

Is Global Warming a Threat?

Islamic Fundamentalism

Organ Transplants

Pandemics

Policing the Internet

Political Activism

Private Character in the Public Eye

Sexually Transmitted Diseases

Should College Athletes Be Paid?

User-Generated Content

Volunteerism

What Are the Causes of Prostitution?

What Is a Hate Crime?

Will the World Run Out of Fresh Water?

At Issue

I The United Nations

Susan C. Hunnicutt, Book Editor

GREENHAVEN PRESS
An imprint of Thomson Gale, a part of The Thomson Corporation

THOMSON
™
GALE

Detroit • New York • San Francisco • New Haven, Conn. • Waterville, Maine • London

Christine Nasso, *Publisher*
Elizabeth Des Chenes, *Managing Editor*

For more information, contact:
Greenhaven Press
27500 Drake Rd.
Farmington Hills, MI 48331-3535
Or you can visit our Internet site at http://www.gale.com

LIBRARY OF CONGRESS CATALOGING-IN-PUBLICATION DATA

The United Nations / Susan C. Hunnicutt, book editor.
     p. cm. -- (At issue)
   Includes bibliographical references and index.
   ISBN-13: 978-0-7377-3695-3 (hardcover)
   ISBN-13: 978-0-7377-3696-0 (pbk.)
   1. United Nations. I. Hunnicutt, Susan
   JZ4984.5.U536 2007
   341.23--dc22

                                                          2007020691

ISBN-10: 0-7377-3695-X (hardcover)
ISBN-10: 0-7377-3696-8 (pbk.)

Printed in the United States of America
10 9 8 7 6 5 4 3 2 1

Contents

Introduction

"Protection, protection. Above all, that's what people are in need of here."

The pleading words of Mia Farrow reflect the sentiments of many concerning armed conflict in Darfur, in western Sudan, which led to the death of more than two hundred thousand people from 2003 through early 2007, and the displacement from their homes of 2.5 million people. "What everyone feared and predicted was that Darfur's crisis would spread across its border into Chad, and this is precisely what has happened," Farrow told a Voice of America reporter in early 2007. "Eastern Chad is on fire. Chadian villages are on fire. Janjaweed (militias from Sudan) have reached far into Chad and joined with Arab militia in Chad to attack black African villages along the eastern border of Chad."

Farrow, acting as a goodwill ambassador for the United Nations Children's Fund (UNICEF) was asking that a United Nations (UN) peacekeeping force be deployed to Chad, where thousands of Darfur refugees are living, and where violence along the Sudanese border has resulted in the displacement of one hundred thousand Chadians as well. "It [a UN peacekeeping force] should have come in to Darfur," she said.

Many powerful voices, including the voices of the president of the United States and a former U.S. secretary of state, have identified what is happening in Darfur as genocide. Like Farrow, many in the international community, including Britain's prime minister Tony Blair and German chancellor Angela Merkel, have looked to the United Nations for a remedy to the crisis. Specific approaches vary. While Farrow was calling for a peacekeeping force—blue-helmeted UN soldiers on the ground in Chad, and preferably also in Darfur—Blair and Merkel have voiced support for economic sanctions to punish the Sudanese government for its failure to protect its

7

own people. Yet in spite of broad consensus that the present situation is intolerable, and in spite of the fact that a range of options for action are available, it has proven difficult for the United Nations to formulate any response at all, beyond a humanitarian program that has provided some relief for refugees. The killing and the destruction of homes and communities has continued. And as Mia Farrow points out, the number of vulnerable people is growing as the conflict spills into a neighboring country.

China, an ally of the Sudanese government, opposes sanctions and supports Sudan's rejection of a UN peacekeeping force in Darfur. As one of five permanent members of the UN Security Council, China has the power to stop the United Nations from embarking on either course of action. Many Arab and Islamic governments who are members of the General Assembly have also been unwilling to challenge in public the actions of Sudanese president Omar Hassan al-Bashir. This political fault line running through the United Nations has resulted in comparisons with earlier crises in Rwanda and Bosnia, in which the United Nations was unable to prevent genocides because of dissent within the Security Council. As in these conflicts, this has led to questions about whether the United Nations really can play a peacemaking role in the modern world. "By and large victims of war and genocide are served about as well by the UN as earlier generations were by the Kellogg-Briand Pact," Nicholas D. Kristof wrote in 2006, in the *International Herald Tribune*. (Kellogg-Briand was a 1920s treaty that attempted to outlaw warfare.) "Granted, when the UN fails, that simply means that its member states fail, but the upshot is still that when genocide alarm bells tinkle, the places to call are Washington, London and Paris, not New York."

According to its charter, the United Nations was formed "to save succeeding generations from the scourge of war . . . to reaffirm faith in fundamental human rights, in the dignity and worth of the human person, in the equal rights of men and women and of nations large and small ..." Clearly, the founders of the United Nations intended to empower it to act both in a peacekeeping role, and as an advocate for the basic human rights of individuals. But article two of the charter also states that members of the United Nations "shall refrain in their international relations from the threat or use of force against the territorial integrity or political independence of any state, or in any other manner inconsistent with the Purposes of the United Nations." Article two creates a formidable obstacle to UN intervention for any but the most serious of human rights violations. And as the situations in Darfur, Kosovo, and Rwanda make clear, even in cases of genocide, political realities may prevent the United Nations from taking actions that are seen by many as morally necessary.

A Chinese official, speaking to the General Assembly of the United Nations in 2005, made the following statement:

> In the endeavor to reduce and prevent large-scale humanitarian crises, the international community should strictly observe the UN Charter, respect the opinions of the countries or organizations concerned, and explore, to the maximum extent, peaceful settlement within the UN framework and with the authorization of the Security Council. We are against any willful intervention on the ground of rash conclusion that a nation is unable or unwilling to protect its own citizens.

This is clearly a response to those who argue that the international community, through the United Nations, has a "responsibility to protect," in situations such as Darfur, in which a government fails to protect its own citizens, and that failure to act may even make them complicit in genocide.

In a speech on the campus of the University of California, Berkeley, in 2007, Romeo Dallaire, the Canadian general who in 1994 led UN efforts to end the genocide in Rwanda, suggested that the UN Charter and the UN Declaration of Human Rights, give "sovereign rights . . . more credence than the rights of individual citizens." In the case of Rwanda, Dallaire says, there was clear early warning that systematic violence against civilians was being planned, yet the UN failed to respond to his requests for additional support, or to give him authority to act to prevent the killing.

Many, however, including Dallaire, believe that the balance is shifting, and that the rights of individuals will weigh more heavily in shaping the UN's response to future crises, as forces of globalization continue to create a more closely knit and interdependent world. In September 2005 the General Assembly of the United Nations unanimously endorsed the principle of the responsibility to protect. Although it has had little apparent impact on the UN's response to the Darfur crisis, this principle asserts that individual states have a responsibility to protect their populations from genocide, war crimes, ethnic cleansing and crimes against humanity, and that the failure to do so may open the way for outside intervention.

Questions like those embodied in this discussion, about the scope and limits of the United Nations' powers and its responsibilities to keep the peace, protect the rights of individuals, and defend the sovereign rights of states, are at the heart of its identity and its role in the world community. They are a central thread that emerges over and over again in the viewpoints that have been selected to appear in *At Issue: The United Nations*.

1

The United Nations Builds Partnerships for a Better World

Kofi A. Annan

Kofi A. Annan of Ghana was the seventh secretary-general of the United Nations (UN), and the first to be elected from the ranks of UN staff. He served as secretary-general of the UN from January 1997 through December 2006. "In Larger Freedom: Towards Development, Security, and Human Rights for All," from which this selection is excerpted, was Annan's five-year progress report on the United Nations' Millennium Development Goals.

It is in the interest of every country to successfully address the interrelated challenges of security, economic development and human rights. The Millennium Development Goals of the United Nations lay out a plan for building partnerships among nations, recognizing the need for sustained global cooperation in order to accomplish these ends.

In a world of inter-connected threats and opportunities, it is in each country's self-interest that all of these challenges are addressed effectively. Hence, the cause of larger freedom can only be advanced by broad, deep and sustained global cooperation among States. The world needs strong and capable States, effective partnerships with civil society and the private sector, and agile and effective regional and global intergovernmental institutions to mobilize and coordinate collective action. The United Nations [UN] must be reshaped in ways not previously imagined, and with a boldness and speed not previously shown.

Freedom from Want

The last 25 years have seen the most dramatic reduction in extreme poverty the world has ever experienced. Yet dozens of countries have become poorer. More than a billion people still live on less than a dollar a day. Each year, 3 million people die from HIV/AIDS and 11 million children die before reaching their fifth birthday.

Today's is the first generation with the resources and technology to make the right to development a reality for everyone and to free the entire human race from want. There is a shared vision of development. The Millennium Development Goals (MDGs), which range from halving extreme poverty to putting all children into primary school and stemming the spread of infectious diseases such as HIV/AIDS, all by 2015, have become globally accepted benchmarks of broader progress, embraced by donors, developing countries, civil society and major development institutions alike.

The MDGs can be met by 2015—but only if all involved break with business as usual and dramatically accelerate and scale up action now.

The threats to peace and security in the 21st century include not just international war and conflict, but terrorism, weapons of mass destruction, organized crime and civil violence.

In 2005, a "global partnership for development"—one of the MDGs reaffirmed in 2002 at the International Conference on Financing for Development at Monterrey, Mexico and the World Summit on Sustainable Development in Johannesburg, South Africa—needs to be fully implemented. That partnership is grounded in mutual responsibility and accountability—developing countries must strengthen governance, combat corruption, promote private sector–led growth and maximize domestic resources to fund national development strategies, while developed countries must support these efforts through increased development assistance, a new development-oriented trade round and wider and deeper debt relief.

Taking Action to Combat Poverty

The following are priority areas for action in 2005:

- *National strategies*: Each developing country with extreme poverty should by 2006 adopt and begin to implement a national development strategy bold enough to meet the MDG targets for 2015. Each strategy needs to take into account seven broad "clusters" of public investments and policies: gender equality, the environment, rural development, urban development, health systems, education, and science, technology and innovation.

- *Financing for development*: Global development assistance must be more than doubled over the next few years. This does not require new pledges from donor countries, but meeting pledges already made. Each developed country that has not already done so should establish a timetable to achieve the 0.7% target of gross national income for official development assistance no later than 2015, starting with significant increases no later than 2006, and reaching 0.5% by 2009. The increase should be front-loaded through an International Finance Facility, and other innovative sources of financing should be considered for the longer term. The Global Fund to Fight HIV/AIDS, Tuberculosis and Malaria must be fully funded and the resources provided for an expanded comprehensive strategy of prevention and treatment to fight HIV/AIDS. These steps should be supplemented by immediate action to support a series of "Quick Wins"—relatively inexpensive, high-impact initiatives with the potential to generate major short-term gains and save millions of lives, such as free distribution of anti-malarial bednets.

- *Trade*: The Doha round of trade negotiations should fulfil its development promise and be completed no later than 2006. [The Doha round talks subsequently broke down, in July of 2006.] As a first step, Member States should provide duty-free and quota-free market access for all exports from the Least Developed Countries.

- *Debt relief*: Debt sustainability should be redefined as the level of debt that allows a country to achieve the MDGs and to reach 2015 without an increase in debt ratios.

Other Advances Are Needed

New action is also needed to ensure *environmental sustainability*. Scientific advances and technological innovation must be mobilized now to develop tools for mitigating *climate change*, and a more inclusive international framework must be developed for stabilizing greenhouse gas emissions beyond the expiry of the Kyoto Protocol in 2012, with broader participation by all major emitters and both developed and developing countries. Concrete steps are also required on *desertification* and *biodiversity*.

Other priorities for global action include stronger mechanisms for *infectious disease* surveillance and monitoring, a world-wide early warning system on *natural disasters*, support for *science and technology* for development, support for *regional infrastructure* and institutions, reform of *international financial institutions*, and more effective cooperation to manage *migration* for the benefit of all.

Freedom from Fear

While progress on development is hampered by weak implementation, on the security side, despite a heightened sense of threat among many, the world lacks even a basic consensus—and implementation, where it occurs, is all too often contested.

The Secretary-General fully embraces a broad vision of collective security. The threats to peace and security in the 21st century include not just international war and conflict, but terrorism, weapons of mass destruction, organized crime and civil violence. They also include poverty, deadly infectious disease and environmental degradation, since these can have equally catastrophic consequences. All of these threats can cause death or lessen life chances on a large scale. All of them can undermine States as the basic unit of the international system.

Collective security today depends on accepting that the threats each region of the world perceives as most urgent are in fact equally so for all. These are not theoretical issues, but ones of deadly urgency.

Key Collective Security Issues

The United Nations must be transformed into the effective instrument for preventing conflict that it was always meant to be, by acting on several key policy and institutional priorities:

- *Preventing catastrophic terrorism*: States should commit to a comprehensive anti-terrorism strategy based on five pillars: dissuading people from resorting to terrorism or supporting it; denying terrorists access to funds and materials; deterring States from sponsoring terrorism; developing State capacity to defeat terrorism; and defending human rights. They should conclude a com-

15

prehensive convention on terrorism, based on a clear and agreed definition. They should also complete, without delay, the convention for the suppression of acts of nuclear terrorism.

- *Nuclear, chemical and biological weapons*: Progress on both disarmament and non-proliferation are essential. On disarmament, nuclear-weapon States should further reduce their arsenals of non-strategic nuclear weapons and pursue arms control agreements that entail not just dismantlement but irreversibility, reaffirm their commitment to negative security assurances, and uphold the moratorium on nuclear test explosions. On non-proliferation, the International Atomic Energy Agency's verification authority must be strengthened through universal adoption of the Model Additional Protocol, and States should commit themselves to complete, sign and implement a fissile material cut-off treaty.

- *Reducing the prevalence and risk of war*: Currently, half the countries emerging from violent conflict revert to conflict within five years. Member States should create an inter-governmental Peacebuilding Commission, as well as a Peacebuilding Support Office within the UN Secretariat, so that the UN system can better meet the challenge of helping countries successfully complete the transition from war to peace. They should also take steps to strengthen collective capacity to employ the tools of mediation, sanctions and peacekeeping (including a "zero tolerance" policy on sexual exploitation of minors and other vulnerable people by members of peacekeeping contingents, to match the policy enacted by the Secretary-General).

- *Use of force*: The Security Council should adopt a resolution setting out the principles to be applied in decisions relating to the use of force and express its intention to be guided by them when deciding whether to authorize or mandate the use of force.

Other priorities for global action include more effective cooperation to combat *organized crime*, to prevent illicit trade in *small arms and light weapons*, and to remove the scourge of *landmines* which still kill and maim innocent people and hold back development in nearly half the world's countries.

Freedom to Live in Dignity

In the Millennium Declaration, Member States said they would spare no effort to promote democracy and strengthen the rule of law, as well as respect for all internationally recognized human rights and fundamental freedoms. And over the last six decades, an impressive treaty-based normative framework has been advanced.

But without implementation, these declarations ring hollow. Without action, promises are meaningless. People who face war crimes find no solace in the unimplemented words of the Geneva Conventions. Treaties prohibiting torture are cold comfort to prisoners abused by their captors, particularly if the international human rights machinery enables those responsible to hide behind friends in high places. War-weary populations despair when, even though a peace agreement has been signed, there is little progress towards government under the rule of law. Solemn commitments to strengthen democracy remain empty words to those who have never voted for their rulers, and who see no sign that things are changing.

Therefore, the normative framework that has been so impressively advanced over the last six decades must be strengthened. Even more important, concrete steps are required to reduce selective application, arbitrary enforcement and breach without consequence. The world must move from an era of legislation to implementation.

Action is called for in the following priority areas:

- *Rule of law*: The international community should embrace the "responsibility to protect", as a basis for collective action against genocide, ethnic cleansing and crimes against humanity. All treaties relating to the protection of civilians should be ratified and implemented. Steps should be taken to strengthen cooperation with the International Criminal Court and other international or mixed war crimes tribunals, and to strengthen the International Court of Justice. The Secretary-General also intends to strengthen the Secretariat's capacity to assist national efforts to re-establish the rule of law in conflict and post-conflict societies.

- *Human rights*: The Office of the High Commissioner for Human Rights should be strengthened with more resources and staff, and should play a more active role in the deliberations of the Security Council and of the proposed Peacebuilding Commission. The human rights treaty bodies of the UN system should also be rendered more effective and responsive.

- *Democracy*: A Democracy Fund should be created at the UN to provide assistance to countries seeking to establish or strengthen their democracy.

Strengthening the United Nations

While purposes should be firm and constant, practice and organization need to move with the times. If the UN is to be a useful instrument for its Member States, and for the world's peoples, in responding to the challenges laid out in the previous ... parts, it must be fully adapted to thee needs and circumstances of the 21st century.

A great deal has been achieved since 1997 in reforming the internal structures and culture of the United Nations. But many more changes are needed, both in the executive branch—the Secretariat and the wider UN system—and in the UN's intergovernmental organs:

- *General Assembly*: The General Assembly should take bold measures to streamline its agenda and speed up the deliberative process. It should concentrate on the major substantive issues of the day, and establish mechanisms to engage fully and systematically with civil society.

- *Security Council*: The Security Council should be broadly representative of the realities of power in today's world. The Secretary-General supports the principles for reform set out in the report of the High-level Panel, and urges Member States to consider the two options, Models A and B, presented in that report, or any other viable proposals in terms of size and balance that have emerged on the basis of either Model. Member States should agree to take a decision on this important issue before the Summit in September 2005.

- *Economic and Social Council*: The Economic and Social Council should be reformed so that it can effectively assess progress in the UN's development agenda, serve as a high-level development cooperation forum, and provide direction for the efforts of the various intergovernmental bodies in the economic and social area throughout the UN system.

- *Proposed Human Rights Council*: The Commission on Human Rights suffers from declining credibility and professionalism, and is in need of major reform. It should be replaced by a smaller standing Human Rights Council, as a principal organ of the United Nations or subsidiary of the General Assembly, whose members would be elected directly by the General Assembly, by a two-thirds majority of members present and voting.

- *The Secretariat*: The Secretary-General will take steps to re-align the Secretariat's structure to match the priorities outlined in the report, and will create a cabinet-style decision-making mechanism. He requests Member States to give him the authority and resources to pursue a one-time staff buy-out to refresh and re-align staff to meet current needs, to cooperate in a comprehensive review of budget and human resources rules, and to commission a comprehensive review of the Office of Internal Oversight Services to strengthen its independence and authority.

Other priorities include creating better system coherence by strengthening the role of *Resident Coordinators*, giving the *humanitarian response system* more effective stand-by arrangements, and ensuring better protection of *internally displaced people*. *Regional organizations*, particularly the African Union, should be given greater support. The Charter itself should also be updated to abolish the *"enemy clauses,"* the *Trusteeship Council* and the *Military Staff Committee*, all of which are outdated.

Opportunity and Challenge

It is for the world community to decide whether this moment of uncertainty presages wider conflict, deepening inequality and the erosion of the rule of law, or is used to renew institutions for peace, prosperity and human rights. Now is the time to act. The annex to the report lists specific items for consideration by Heads of State and Government. Action on them is possible. It is within reach. From pragmatic beginnings could emerge a visionary change of direction for the world.

2

The True Purpose of the United Nations Is Totalitarian Rule

Dennis Behreandt

Dennis Behreandt writes regularly for the New American, *a publication of the John Birch Society. The John Birch Society has criticized U.S. involvement in the United Nations for decades.*

The United Nations (UN) has all the elements of a government, similar to the structure of the U.S. government. A close look at its history reveals that it was always intended by its founders to become a world governing body. Although the UN seeks to be known as the world's most important humanitarian organization, it is in fact the bureaucratic instrument of a global state with totalitarian aspirations.

The United Nations has been portrayed as the world's most important humanitarian organization. The propaganda supporting this view has been continuous for so long that few doubt the depiction. When disasters such as the devastating Asian tsunami occur, the UN and its pundits are quick to position the world body in the limelight with pronouncements depicting the organization as the leading supplier and coordinator of relief and aid.

Such a picture of the UN as merely a helpful relief and humanitarian agency is dangerously deceptive and inaccurate.

Dennis Behreandt, "Framework for World Government: From the Moment State Department Planners in the Roosevelt Administration Began Crafting Plans for the United Nations, Their Goal Was Always the Same: World Government," *New American*, vol. 21, July 11, 2005, pp. 13–15. Copyright © 2005 American Opinion Publishing Incorporated. Reproduced by permission.

It is true that the world body does participate in relief efforts when disasters occur, but this is only the public face of the organization. A clear-eyed survey of the makeup of the UN, though, finds that the world body is much more than a relief organization. It has, for instance, a clearly delineated executive branch in the office of the secretary-general. It has a similarly delineated legislative branch in the General Assembly and Security Council. And it has subsidiaries and affiliates, like the World Court, the nascent International Criminal Court, and certain tribunals, that function as a judiciary branch.

Those familiar with the composition of governing bodies will recognize in this structure the basic framework of government. And this is precisely what the United Nations is and always has been. In fact, from the very moment of its birth during and immediately following the great upheaval of World War II, the true purpose of the United Nations has been obscured. Born in secrecy while the world convulsed in the violence of war, the founders of the world body, primarily found in the subversive and internationalist ranks of the Council on Foreign Relations [an influential foreign policy think tank] labored to lay the groundwork for world government. The United Nations was designed from the beginning to be the instrument through which they would achieve this dangerous goal.

Prewar Planning

On December 22, 1941, just two weeks after the Japanese attack on Pearl Harbor, British and U.S. officials met in Washington, D.C., to discuss matters pertaining to war. The discussions, dubbed the Arcadia Conference, lasted until January 14, 1942. During the talks, British Prime Minister Winston Churchill pushed for aggressive military action and agreed with U.S. officials and President Franklin Delano Roosevelt on a "beat Germany first" strategy. Roosevelt, for his part, began immediately to lay the groundwork for the post-war world by presenting a draft for a "Declaration of the United Nations."

This early declaration was perceived at the time as providing the Allied powers with a formal, unified front from which to face the dangers posed by Nazi Germany, Imperial Japan, and the other Axis nations. Nevertheless, it contained in broad outline the foundation for what would become the world body. The fact that the draft declaration was available just a few short weeks after the bombing of Pearl Harbor suggests that the document had, in fact, been in the works for some time prior to the entry of the United States into the war.

In fact, work to lay the foundation for a new international order had begun some years earlier and was carried out by key Roosevelt adviser Sumner Welles. A devotee of former President [Woodrow] Wilson, Welles was a dedicated internationalist and member at a young age of the Council on Foreign Relations (CFR). The CFR was an outgrowth of efforts to form a new international order after the failure by the Wilson administration to get us into the League of Nations [an organization similar to the United Nations, established in 1919]. Since that time, the CFR has pushed the world government line.

Roosevelt and his internationalist confederates were determined to use the war to submerge the U.S. and other independent nations in a system of world government.

In 1937 Welles, then undersecretary of state, proposed what came to be called his "American System" through which he thought it would be possible to create "a new world order." According to the book *Sumner Welles, Postwar Planning, and the Quest for a New World Order 1937–1943* by Christopher D. O'Sullivan, professor of history at the University of San Francisco, Welles proposed that Roosevelt "call for sweeping arms reductions, the lowering of international trade barriers and the unity of the neutral powers in quarantining aggressor nations."

The Plan Moves Forward

When war engulfed Europe in 1939, Welles and other Roosevelt administration internationalists sensed an opportunity to use the fighting to advance plans for a new world order. The U.S., though, was not yet in the war, and it would seem out of place, the administration thought, for the U.S. government to begin official efforts at postwar planning. Such planning would need to be initiated outside of official government offices. Naturally, CFR member Sumner Welles looked to the council for help. According to O'Sullivan, "A few weeks after the outbreak of war, he asked Hamilton Fish Armstrong, the director of the Council on Foreign Relations, to prepare for him a number of detailed studies on postwar planning."

Shortly afterward but still in 1939, Welles assembled a committee within the State Department to study postwar planning. The Welles Advisory Committee on Problems of Foreign Relations was singularly concerned with world order. According to the State Department, the body would "survey the basic principles which should underlie a desirable world order to be evolved after the termination of present hostilities." The committee would also "determine policies which should be pursued by the United States in furtherance of the establishment of such a world order."

Roosevelt and his internationalist confederates were determined to use the war to submerge the U.S. and other independent nations in a system of world government. On July 22, 1941, Welles made the administration's aims clear in a speech broadcast by radio throughout the nation and occupied Europe. The U.S., he said, would seek a replacement for the League of Nations. "I cannot believe that peoples of goodwill will not once more strive to realize the great ideal of an association of nations through which the freedom, happiness, and the security of all peoples may be achieved. That is the objective before us all today—to try and find the means of bringing that to pass." In short, Welles had announced, said historian O'Sullivan, "that American war aims should seek to forever change the global status quo. He desired a postwar settlement based not on great-power politics and the balance of power but on a universal vision of a new world order."

The Atlantic Charter

In August 1941, President Roosevelt secretly met with British Prime Minister Winston Churchill. Roosevelt was to negotiate with Churchill an agreement that would firmly align the United States with Britain both for wartime purposes and for the postwar world. The result of the meeting was published on August 14, 1941 as the Atlantic Charter. Welles desperately wanted the charter to include explicit mention of a system of world order, and the original draft of the charter did call for the creation of "an effective international organization." Both Welles and Churchill pushed for the inclusion of such language, but Roosevelt, fearing a domestic backlash if the wording was left in, stood fast on its removal, inserting instead an oblique reference to the future "establishment of a wider and permanent system of general security."

The Atlantic Charter was the kernel around which the United Nations was formed. That its aim was the submergence of sovereign states, including the United States, under an all-powerful world government was ably explained as early as February 13, 1943 by New York Congressman Joseph Clark Baldwin. Baldwin, a supporter of the charter, explained how under its terms national sovereignty would be diminished. "Local police forces . . . obviously should be reduced as state and national police protection is increased," Baldwin said in a speech to the Foreign Policy Association of Pennsylvania. "So our national armed forces can and should be reduced as soon as a permanent international police force is set up."

The United Nations Is Born

With this groundwork in place well before the attack at Pearl Harbor, the Roosevelt administration was well positioned to move forward with postwar planning for what would become the United Nations. Beginning with the aforementioned Arcadia Conference in Washington, D.C., on December 22. 1941, plans to build the UN began accelerating. At Arcadia, 26 nations agreed to the terms of the Atlantic Charter, the group being christened for the first time by Roosevelt as the United Nations.

Arcadia, though, was just the formal beginning of the process that resulted in the UN. Even before Pearl Harbor, Sumner Welles had been asking Roosevelt to authorize yet another secret committee to formulate plans for the creation of and U.S. participation in an international governing organization. Roosevelt apparently agreed, and Secretary of State Cordell Hull assumed the role of chairman of the new committee. When Hull took his annual leave, though, at the beginning of 1942, Sumner Welles, the undersecretary of state, found that the other appointments to the committee had not yet been made. Sensing an opportunity to pack the committee with like-minded CFR internationalists, Welles set about sending invitations. When he was through, the new Advisory Committee on Post-War Foreign Policy (later the Informal Agenda Group) would include a who's who of committed one-world internationalists from the CFR. Welles appointed himself head of the group's subcommittee in charge of defining the nature of a postwar international organization. To that end, he proposed, in March 1942, the creation of a "United Nations authoritative body."

The United Nations has continued down to the present to be used by one-worlders to build world government.

Under the general oversight of Secretary of State Hull, Sumner's committees completed their work during 1942 and 1943. According to historian Christopher O'Sullivan, Sumner's work "included an examination of other international organizations (with special attention paid to the League of Nations), the drafting of a constitution for the new world body, a detailed examination of international trusteeship and, later, formulating suggestions on how to endow a new world organization with a military capability. During its existence the subcommittee on international organization would succeed in creating the blueprint for a new world body that would evolve into the United Nations."

The New World Order

Strictly speaking, the Welles-Roosevelt-CFR plan for a new world order came to fruition with the founding conference of the UN in San Francisco in 1945. Significantly, the secretary-general of the conference was none other than Soviet spy Alger Hiss. But Hiss was far from the only Communist or Communist sympathizer to be heavily involved in the creation of the UN. Moreover, Communist interest in the world body pointed toward its true purpose. After all, Communists were and are dedicated to creating a one-world Communist superstate. Their heavy involvement in the world body's founding is a powerful indictment of that organization's true purpose as a nascent world government.

The United Nations has continued down to the present to be used by one-worlders to build world government. Though leaders have been comparatively circumspect about their goals in recent decades, suggestive and sometimes explicit statements are still made.

For example, Kofi Annan [the secretary-general of the UN from 1997 to 2006] views the UN as an instrument of global government. On January 14, 2000, Annan lauded the work of the UN in creating "a framework of international law," before going on to say: "Local communities have their fire departments and town councils. Nations have their courts and legislatures. In today's interdependent world, the peoples of the world must have the rules and institutions they need to manage their lives." At a press conference in 1999, he was even more explicit, saying, "every community needs rules. The international community needs them as much as a local community or a district. . . . [T]he challenge on the global level—what I will call global governance—is something that is going to confront us all very, very starkly."

Should the trend toward world government initiated by Sumner Welles and other internationalists during World War II continue unabated, the world will indeed have peace, the kind of peace that comes under the iron grip of a world-spanning totalitarian bureaucracy.

3

Many Americans Have an Inaccurate Impression of the United Nations

John Tessitore

John Tessitore is executive editor of the Carnegie Council and oversees all print and electronic media, including the Council's journal Ethics in International Affairs. *He also is a communications consultant to several United Nations (UN) agencies. From 1985 to 2002, he was executive director of communications for the United Nations Association of the United States.*

The United Nations evokes strong and differing feelings among the American public, in part because Americans do not have good sources of information. American public school textbooks include very little information about the founding or the work of the United Nations. Objective television news coverage about the UN's involvement in world affairs is almost totally absent, while intensely held editorial opinions appear frequently. The result is a great many misconceptions about the United Nations and its work. Americans need better information about the United Nations because the future of the UN deserves serious consideration.

A S UNITED NATIONS Secretary-General Ban Kimoon assumes leadership of one of the world's oldest and most visible international forums [in 2007], the old French phrase "plus ca change, plus c'est la meme chose" ("the more things change, more they remain the same") comes curiously to mind. Will a new U.N. head really make a difference in the seemingly endless love-hate relationship between the U.S. and the U.N.?

Indeed, it seems remarkable that an organization that has now been in existence for fully six decades continues to invoke such strong, visceral, and competing responses from the American public—from a sort of nostalgic veneration (particularly from older Americans who remember the promise of its founding at the end of World War II) to an almost hysterical vilification (in general, by the political right), in which the world body is blamed for virtually every act of global inequity and malfeasance—including, of course, illegal parking on the streets of New York City.

While it is crucial that the U.N. continue to evolve and to reform—something it has done continually since its founding—it is also crucial that it be better understood. To this end, perhaps the U.N.'s greatest shortcoming has been in public relations. The simple fact is, in 60 years it has done an absolutely terrible job of explaining to the American public exactly what it is and what it does. Oh, yes, we all think we know what it is and what it does. But where does our information come from?

A recent study of American public-school textbooks showed that there is virtually nothing taught about the United Nations in our classrooms beyond that it was founded in 1945. A paragraph or two at most. As to television news, long gone are the days when the national networks actually covered the United Nations. Americans over 50 might dimly recall veteran CBS correspondent Richard C. Hottelett reporting nightly (!) from U.N. Headquarters, the flags blowing behind him on First Avenue (in black and white, of course). But that was nearly a half-century ago.

Today, we no longer have reporting on the United Nations, we have judgments on the U.N.—and these judgments are good or bad, depending largely upon the editorial perspective of the news agency or the political affiliation of the commentator. For example, the so-called "Oil-for-Food scandal," in which a small number of U.N. officials were accused of corruption in overseeing the sale of Iraqi oil in exchange for much-needed food and medical supplies, generated countless anti-U.N. and, more particularly, anti-Secretary Gen. Kofi Annan articles (inasmuch as a personal figure always makes the drama that much more sensational). One of the loudest members of the U.N. lynch mob was Claudia Rosett, a former member of *The Wall Street Journal* editorial board—a group known for its enmity toward the U.N. and any other organization that might threaten to curtail U.S. unilateralism.

Ms. Rosett, who now identifies herself as a journalist-in-residence at the rather paranoid-sounding "Foundation for Defense of Democracies," recently addressed the Providence Committee on Foreign Relations on the Oil-for-Food scandal (which she takes credit for having revealed) and called for not simply the reform of the organization but for complete U.S. withdrawal. When a distinguished member of the audience pointed out that the United States was itself complicit in the so-called scandal, her response was that we should withdraw from the U.N. because we should not belong to an organization that would tempt us to behave in such a manner!

Such tortured reasoning would be comical if it were not for the fact that there are some who actually take such comments seriously. Of course, by extension such logic would mean that the U.S. must cease to do business with Halliburton [controversial, lucrative defense contractor with ties to Vice President Dick Cheney] immediately, but that is not part of Ms. Rosett's or *The Wall Street Journal's* agenda.

So what are some of the myths and misconceptions that continue to prevent the American public from better understanding the complicated and sometimes delicate U.S.-U.N. relationship? Briefly, they are these:

- The United Nation[s] is not a world government. Indeed, it is not a government of any kind. It is simply a meeting place, where the nations of the world attempt to conduct their business in the same competitive, se[l]f-serving, and even (dare we say) deceitful way that they always have and surely always will. The one difference is that everyone is in the same place at the same time, which makes for obvious economies.

- The United Nations has no standing army. In fact, it does not possess one gun, one troop, one armored vehicle. All the ordnance and every blue-helmeted soldier is loaned to the U.N. by a sovereign nation and under the command of professional military officer[s]— largely, by the way, drawn from among U.S. allies (Ireland, India, Pakistan, Australia, Canada, to name a few).

- The secretary-general does not have the power to create a peacekeeping mission. That power rests with the Security Council alone. Further, in the entire 60-year history of the United Nations, no Security Council resolution (and thus no peacekeeping mission) has ever been passed without the consent of the United States. Why? Very simple: The U.S. is one of five countries with veto power.

- The U.N. has made peace where the U.S. and other nations have failed. Over the past two decades the U.N. has brokered the peace of inter-state and civil wars all over the world, including many that defied all U.S. efforts at mediation (Iran-Iraq, USSR-Afghanistan, El Salvador, etc.). In so doing, it also won the Nobel Peace Prize—seven times.

- The U.S. does not pay most of the U.N. budget. Contrary to a very popular misconception, the U.S. actually pays less than its fair share of the U.N. budget—22 percent—based on an agreed upon formula that considers the wealth of each nation. Japan, with a much smaller economy, pays nearly 20 percent.

What's next for the U.S. and the U.N.? A fair question. And an important one. It deserves thoughtful consideration.

4

The United Nations Must Reform Its Management Practices

Mohammad Tal

Mohammad Tal is first secretary at the Jordan mission to the United Nations.

In recent years, the United Nations has been asked to address an increasing number of issues, and to find solutions to an expanding range of problems. However, the process of adding responsibilities has not been an orderly one. Communication between stakeholders has been flawed, generating mistrust, and new areas of involvement have not been integrated into a comprehensive plan for financial management of resources. Efforts to reform the United Nations must focus on the organization's management practices, in order to rebuild the confidence of stakeholders.

In September 2005, the General Assembly of the United Nations held an exceptional session attended by a large number of heads of States and governments to evaluate the work of the organization in the past 60 years and agree on a strategic vision to guide it in the future. Many were skeptical about this Summit as being "just another high profile meeting," but in essence, the World Summit of 2005 was an opportunity for Member States to reflect on the current state of affairs at the UN and initiate a reform roadmap to take the organization into the 21st century.

Mohammad Tal, "United Nations Management Reform: A Perspective," *Global Policy Forum*, February 4, 2007. Reproduced by permission.

While the resolution adopted at the World Summit[1] addressed a multitude of subjects, there was a nagging need to devote special attention to the areas of management and administration. Management reform was seen by many as the most important element in the overall UN reform equation. Not only because it is directly linked to financial resources but also because the overall future success of the organization may very well depend on its ability to adopt genuine and sustainable managerial and administrative reforms. In this context, one can firmly argue that failure to take progressive measures in the areas of management and administration would undermine other reforms in the organization and put to question the credibility of the UN and its future role as the World's supreme multilateral body.

As one attempts to understand the dilemma of UN management reform, one must keep in mind that the recent commitment of the world leaders as contained in the World Summit Outcome document is only one episode in the reform efforts that started almost a decade ago. Secretary General Kofi Annan launched an enthusiastic campaign to address issues related to management and financing reforms as early as 1997 and submitted a series of reports[2] for the consideration of the General Assembly. In the Millennium Declaration the GA resolved "to ensure that the organization is provided on a timely and predictable basis with the resources it needs to carry out its mandates"[3] and urged "the Secretariat to make the best use of those resources."[4]

1. The World Summit Outcome Document contained in General Assembly Resolution A/Res./60/1.
2. Reports such as those contained in A/51/950 (Renewing the United Nations: A program for reform); A/53/98 (United Nations reform: Measures and proposals); A/54/2000 (We the people,: The role of the United Nations in the 21st century); A/57/387 (Strengthening of the United Nations: An agenda for further change) among others and their corresponding resolutions may not have been management reform specific. Yet, they served to inform Member States and those concerned of the need to address this issue. More recently, the General Assembly debated a series of management reform specific reports as it considered different items on its agenda.
3. Millennium Declaration A/Res./55/2.
4. Millennium Declaration A/Res./55/2.

Since then, the issue of management reform started taking center stage and reform efforts were reported to the Assembly regularly as part of the reporting on various agenda items.[5]

As this "management reform fever" swept the United Nations, it was constantly accompanied by endless debates and discussions regarding the division of labor between the Secretariat and Member States. On the one hand, Member States felt that their position as the "ultimate decision makers" in the organization was being compromised by some of the proposed changes and thus argued against them. On the other hand, the Secretariat constantly accused Member States of "micro management" and argued that it was deprived of the tools to carry out its management responsibilities efficiently and effectively. Interestingly enough both arguments were valid to an extent and the reciprocal feelings of unease evolved into a general sentiment of distrust.

Member states have mandated the United Nations to deal with a multitude of issues.

In this context, it must be acknowledged that introducing organizational change of any kind is always uncomfortable. Change entails uncertainty for the stakeholders with regard to future rights, responsibilities, privileges and roles and because of this very reason, reform efforts must be transparent and participatory in nature. As we embark on an effort to reform management at the UN, we must be fully cognizant of the magnitude of the challenge the UN is up against. Anything short of a full understanding of such challenge would hinder our ability to reach sustainable solutions and render our efforts obsolete.

5. Several agenda items that dealt with financial and budgetary matters included reform elements. For example, there were reports dealing with reforming Human Resources Management, Procurement, Provision of Conference Services, Oversight functions, Planning and Budgeting among others presented to the Assembly and in many cases the GA either pronounced itself on some of the proposals contained in such reports or sought additional information from the Secretariat.

The Essence of the Problem

It is no secret that the United Nations today is a much different organization than the one established in 1945. The UN's agenda expanded tremendously in recent years and its focus is no longer strictly political or economic. Member States have mandated the United Nations to deal with a multitude of issues and find solutions to problems ranging from preservation of international peace and security to promoting sustainable economic development to poverty and disease eradication as well as peace building and the promotion of human rights. One would only need to consider the exponential expansion in the UN's financing requirements to realize the extent of the vast responsibilities that Member States entrusted the UN with. The United Nations regular budget increased from $2.6 billion in the biennial 1996–1997 to $3.6 billion in the biennial 2004–2005. Peace keeping operations budgets expanded at a faster pace from $2.2 billion to over $9.4 billion for the same period as the number of missions increased. All in all, the total resources available to the organization including extra budgetary[6] funds doubled between the biennial 1996–1997 and 2004–2005 to reach $18.5 billion.[7]

This vast expansion in mandates and responsibilities necessitated an increase in staff at all levels both for substantive and support activities. The UN also underwent changes in management structures, human resource policies, information technology, procurement and security requirements, to name a few. In many ways, the UN could not afford to be a static organization any more and needed to evolve into an agile body with rapid deployment capabilities and a multidisciplinary expert staff that is capable of handling the wide range of issues on its agenda. However, this rapid pace of change in

6. Extra budgetary resources are basically voluntary contributions and other funding mechanisms outside the scope of the regular budget. The regular budget is assessed to member states on an annual basis.
7. The Secretary General's report "Investing in the United Nations: for a stronger organization worldwide" contained in document A/60/692, figure 3, pg. 10.

responsibilities as mandated by Member States far exceeded the ability of the organization keep up. The Secretariat exerted tremendous efforts to handle the new reality but found that its efforts were no match to the continuous increase in the workload. One could even argue that the rapid rate of change in the organization made long term strategic planning difficult especially with the old management tools the UN had at its disposal. The Secretariat's mode of operation was reactionary in nature and while that mode may have served a short term requirement or fulfilled an immediate need, it led the organization into becoming a classic bureaucracy with multiple layers of management, parallel lines of reporting, overlapping responsibilities and structures as well as a complete absence of effective responsibility and accountability mechanisms. In its attempt to keep up, the Secretariat submitted proposal after proposal on financial and management issues for the consideration of and decision by the General Assembly but such proposals were often unclear, incomplete and lacked proper justification. Naturally, they did not enjoy the support of the Assembly especially if they entailed additional financial appropriations.

As much as one is tempted to think that the United Nations could have done better in managing its added responsibilities within the resources it had, it is difficult to ignore the financial constraint imposed on the organization and assume that added efficiency could have replaced the need for more resources. It remains disturbing that Member States were quite generous when it came to entrusting the United Nations to implement new mandates yet, allowed very little growth in its regular budget. The expansion of the agenda of some of the UN's main organs could have never been financed from the "existing resources" of the organization. This cliché which plagued many GA resolutions on budgeting and management was the way member states naively thought they could impose fiscal discipline on the organization. Clearly, fiscal discipline was not realized as the organization drifted into higher levels of inefficiency.

It is of no surprise therefore that "lack of resources" was [cited] repeatedly in the report of the Secretary General "Investing in the United Nations: for a stronger Organization worldwide" as the reason why the organization could not have done better in different areas. The organization grew to rely on extra budgetary resources as a mechanism to help it keep up with new demands despite the fact that such resources were meant to compl[e]ment regular budgetary allocations rather than replace them. Member States chose to be in denial of the need to increase the resources available to the organization and a couple of decades later realized that the status quo cannot be maintained. The stakeholders are now convinced that management reform at this stage is a must but it will be costly, time consuming and politically more difficult.

In essence, the current management state of affairs in the United Nations is a natural outcome of an interaction process between the Secretariat and Member States that can at best be characterized by relative unease, lack of cooperation and deep distrust. The Secretariat failed to provide Member States with the full and necessary information for proper decision making. Lack of clarity of the Secretariat's proposals and weak justifications reinforced the General Assembly's fear of losing control and glorified its suspicion of "hidden agendas." In the eyes of many Member States, the Secretariat disregarded their directives and was selective in implementing their mandates. Having said that, Member States also contributed to the deteriorating situation since their discussions shifted from substance to political posturing and score settling. The consultations the GA held on management and budgetary matters were reduced to endless debates over the allocation of posts and more often reciprocating of blames. It is even more disturbing that the outcome of such endless debates reflected the lowest common denominator of positions which rendered the resolutions vague and difficult to implement. On a slightly different but certainly relevant note, some Member States could not make up their mind regarding the independence of the Secretariat and the preservation of article 100 of the charter. Despite the repeated pronouncements to the contrary, major financial contributors could not resist the temptation of intervention and the exertion of influence on the Secretariat whenever possible.

The end result was the subordination of the interest of the United Nations to that of individual Member States or regional groups. The membership of this organization failed to realize the fact that the supreme interest of the United Nations is above and beyond the narrow mathematical sum of the so called interest of membership. For management reforms to succeed, reform effort must focus on this fact. Reforming management at the United Nations is a collective responsibility and as such, no one party can claim credit for it. Equally so, failure to achieve management reform is a collective failure and no regional group can be singled out and blamed for it.

A Closer Look at the Current Reform Efforts

The United Nations has been the subject of a great deal of criticism and attacks in the last few years. The organization was plagued by many scandals that touched the very core of the organization's reputation and credibility. The Oil for Food scandal and the multiple reports of sexual or financial misconduct on the part of UN personnel in Peace Keeping Operations and at headquarters put the UN in a very peculiar position. These scandals raised concerns not only about the ability of the UN to sustain and deliver but also put to question its role in the future. While the need to take swift action against those who were responsible for the scandals was never greater, many felt that the UN's handling of such scandals did not match their gravity. Launching independent investigative efforts or suspending the service of some personnel was considered by many as nothing more than a slap on the wrist. While the political will to take swift action was not really put to question, many questions were raised about the reasons behind the continuation of such violations and more so about the ability of the UN to prevent them or handle them if they occur. As the UN navigated through the rough waters of media campaigns and membership's calls for accountability and better management, the UN had to launch a counter offensive. This counter offensive aimed at restoring its credibility and role and thus, had to address all aspects of the organization's work including issues such as accountability, responsibility, oversight, internal controls, and delegation of authority. There is no doubt that the World Summit of 2005 was part of this counter offensive to restore the credibility and reputation of the United Nations. The Outcome document of 2005 served to reiterate the consensus of the world leaders that the UN not only should be maintained and strengthened but also that specific steps will be taken to achieve this end.

Unfortunately, the credibility of the organization could not be restored by the mere adoption of a document. Delegations realized that their linguistic exercise to reach an agreement on the elements contained in the Outcome document was only the tip of the iceberg since the serious work would only start when the vision of the document would be implemented. As far as management issues and related topics, the Outcome document was limited to general principles that may have appeared previously in past resolutions or other UN documents. Even the specific section that dealt with management reforms was nothing but a statement of good intentions and not one that was detailed enough to provide a clear road map. The stance of the document weakened as events unfolded in the last few months of 2005 especially with the results of the 2006–2007 biennial budget negotiations along with the inability or unwillingness of Member States to reach a solid agreement on the specifics of the process ahead. But then it would have been politically impossible for any party to even question the Outcome document since it became the scripture of the UN and other UN terms of reference including past resolutions were virtually subordinated to it. This rendered the process of management reform more vulnerable to the all too familiar deficient interaction process between the Secretariat and Member States.

In a way, this was not surprising since for change to succeed in any organization let alone one as complex and controversial as the United Nations, it must be gradual, methodically applied, inclusive and collaborative. Unfortunately, the process that led to the adoption of the Outcome document was neither. It was motivated by political pressures by some of the major players, it set artificial deadlines and the negotiations that led to it were less than inclusive in the eyes of many. The nagging question that accompanied this process was whether Member States' end goal was to accomplish genuine reforms in the ways the organization is managed or simply to adopt a document to take back to their capitals claiming that the organization has been reformed. In other words, were the advocates of management reform more interested in the process or the outcome as such distinctly different goals would require distinctly different courses of action.

The predominantly political motivations behind the efforts to reform the UN's management and the deficient process through which some thought management reform could be introduced are the very reasons why the efforts underway in their current format are bound to fail. The political differences and the positions presented at the multiple briefings and side discussions preceding the release of the Secretary General's report "Investing in the United Nations: for a stronger Organization Worldwide," was indicative of the wide gap in the positions of the stakeholders. This gap not only reflected a difference in the assessment of the state of affairs in the organization but also a difference in visions and modalities to achieve the proposed reforms. As one would expect, the issue of financial resources was essentially at the heart of the management reform discussions. Despite the fact that the increase in the financial requirements of the United Nations and the "rising cost of running the organization" was seldom referred to by major contributors like the United States, Japan and the EU, such major contributors were constantly uneasy about it.

In the case of the United States, US representative Henry Hyde of Illinois introduced the "UN reform Legislation" which links US payment of its dues to achieving measurable reforms. In the words of Mr. Hyde, "we are opposed to legendary bureaucratization, to political grandstanding, to billions of dollars spent on a multitude of programs with meager results, to the outright misappropriation of funds represented by the emerging scandal regarding the Oil for Food program." This kind of pressure from national governments prompted representatives of the major contributors to scrutinize every expense and every activity to a point where describing the debates of the General Assembly on budgetary and management matters as Micromanagement would have been an understatement. Clearly, there was a great deal of confusion about the real goal to be achieved since the focus was on reducing budgetary requests by different departments to lower the overall budget level and by extension reduce the burden on member states. Yet this came at the expense of the ability of the organization to deliver in different areas. In essence, lowering the cost of running the organization was constantly confused with realizing higher rates of efficiency even though the two concepts are obviously different. Long term economies of scale and lower cost of operation are an outcome and a direct result of realizing higher rates of efficiency, not the other way around. Unfortunately, the substance of the issue at hand was virtually lost in the endless discussions on the elements contained in the SG's report, its forum of discussion and decision making and how such forum would not duplicate other fora in which some of the topics were to be discussed. Lack of the necessary level of details in the proposals and the clear disconnect between some of them and the contributions they make to improving management at the UN complicated the discussions even further. The General Assembly found itself in an all too familiar situation having to make decisions based on incomplete information. Thus, it reacted in its usual manner seeking additional information and being less forthcoming vis a vis the proposals.

Clearly, the issue of management reform in the United Nations deserves the membership's utmost attention as it is a prerequisite for the future sustenance and survival of the organization.

As the process continues and as Member States embark on a substantive discussion of the recently issued detailed report of the SG on management reform, it is essential that all stakeholders take a step back and carefully reflect on the past few months and think long and hard about how they want to continue this process. If the future discussions on reforming UN management will continue to be motivated by political agendas, financing threats, resistance to change or utter denial of its necessity then it is very difficult to see how real change can be achieved. Reforming management at the United Nations should not be held hostage to threats of withholding the payment of dues and ditching Member States' responsibilities as stipulated in the charter nor should it be a function of some member's aspiration for special status in the organization. At the same time, utter resistance to change and the unjustifiable constant refusal to genuinely engage in the process of management reform would only invite retaliatory behavior and further complicate and politicize the discussions. Genuine change cannot be imposed and real reform can only be brought about if there is a broad agreement on the vision of change and the modalities to achieve it. Resistance is expected but the stakeholders can be motivated to accept it. For this to happen, a truly collaborative effort is needed in which the stakeholders abandon political posturing and stick to sound management principles as their guide to achieving the hoped for results. Only then can the membership claim to have made a contribution to preserving the organization, its role and credibility as the supreme multilateral body in the world.

Conclusion

Clearly, the issue of management reform in the United Nations deserves the membership's utmost attention as it is a prerequisite for the future sustenance and survival of the organization. It is both complex and sensitive and while I have advocated a "sound management" approach to fixing the current deficiencies, the intergovernmental nature of the organization must always be taken into account. Ignoring this fact will only perpetrate more complications and further threaten potential achievements. Politics and special interests will always be variables in the reform equation but it is up to the membership to decide what is a priority for them; scoring menial points and reciprocating blames or uplifting the organization to a higher standard that is worthy of its role. While the reform efforts of the past have been fragmented and many reform processes ran in parallel, their results must be thoroughly analyzed and reasons for failure completely understood. Launching a reform vision that ignores past efforts and does not address the concerns of all stakeholders will never translate into reality.

In the end, the United Nations is not a random entity that evolved into its current form but rather one that was created, financed and mandated by its members to take certain actions or conduct certain tasks. By their very nature, legislative processes are arduous, time consuming and in the eyes of many, relatively inefficient. Yet, I do not think we have heard voices advocating giving up such processes because they take too long or cost too much. What is also of grave concern is the perpetuation of the notion that the United Nations is this hideous organization that is out there to waste international taxpayers' money. As absurd as that notion is, one finds many willing to entertain it and use it as a way to criticize the organization and create an impression of its failure. To the best of our knowledge, the United Nations has not failed. It has lived up to the expectations of its members and repeatedly fulfilled the mandates it was entrusted with. For those who feel that the UN's role can be replaced by regional arrangements or otherwise, it is difficult to think of a single organization that can be created today with expertise in the diverse areas that the UN is involved in. Therefore, preservation of the United Nations should be the priority of all of its members as every member regardless of size or financial contribution stands everything to lose if the United Nations is compromised in the future.

It must also be kept in mind that management reform is a long process and gradualism is a virtue in this case. Despite the frustrations of different members about the way the organization is run and the pressures that such members are subjected to by their national constituencies, changing the way the organization is run will take time. Emphasis should be placed on launching a focused effort and sustaining it long enough to [bear] its fruits. Any illusion that there is a fast track approach to management reform will prove to be nothing but an illusion. It remains to be seen whether the membership and the Secretariat are collectively willing to rise up to the responsibility and take the necessary steps to change the organization or just settle for another round of endless discussions with marginal contribution to improving management in the organization.

5

The UN Needs to Shift from Peacekeeping to Peace Building

Crispin Grey-Johnson

Crispin Grey-Johnson is permanent representative of Gambia to the United Nations. He has served Gambia as ambassador to Brazil, the Ivory Coast, Liberia, the United States, and Venezuela, and as high commissioner to Canada and Sierra Leone. Grey-Johnson has published extensively on African employment, education, and development issues.

The United Nations [UN] often intervenes in trouble spots throughout the world to bring an end to conflict. However, these efforts frequently fall short of addressing the root causes of violence, and thus do not result in a lasting peace. Genuine peace building requires restoration of political authority, economic stability, and a functioning justice system. In order to build lasting peace, issues of governance must be addressed.

Peacekeeping has occupied a central place in United Nations activities in the last decade or so and was given added prominence following the adoption in 2000 of the Report of the Panel on United Nations Peace Operations, known as the Brahimi Report.

Scores of peacekeeping missions have been mounted in trouble spots worldwide; in Africa, the majority of operations

Crispin Grey-Johnson, "Beyond Peacekeeping: The Challenges of Post-Conflict Reconstruction and Peacebuilding in Africa," *UN Chronicle*, vol. 43, March–May 2006, pp. 8–11. Copyright © 2006 United Nations. Reprinted with the permission of the United Nations.

were conducted in situations of internal conflict. While such intervention has led to cessation of hostilities, it has not necessarily resulted [in] a permanent peace nor has it fully addressed the factors that led to the conflict in the first place. The reasons for this shortcoming have to do with the causes of the conflict, the peacekeeping mandates, the structure and composition of the missions, and the perceived role of the United Nations in mediation. Many conflicts remain only superficially resolved, with all the elements for a relapse remaining intact. In fact, in some countries hostilities flared as soon as the United Nations left, as was the case in the Central African Republic and Haiti.

The United Nations must find a formula that will allow a successful transition from peacekeeping to peacebuilding and consolidation. But it is not presently structured to easily identify where to place this mandate within the Organization. The Security Council's mandate is clearly defined and limited to issues of global security, and peacebuilding goes beyond the need to secure the peace. It encompasses interventions that derive from a development mandate, which is the purview of the Economic and Social Council. This gap has been recognized over the years, leading to serious reflection on what is needed to invest the United Nations with the capability and capacity not only to make the peace but also to maintain and sustain it.

Peacekeeping Defined

UN peacekeeping missions in internal conflicts are mounted when there has been a near-total breakdown of law and order: Governments have lost control; civilians are at the mercy of the warring parties; women, children and other vulnerable groups face extreme hardships; and there appears to be no end in sight. In many cases, government security capabilities would have been completely lost, and peacekeeping missions would be expected to provide security, secure public institutions and perform civilian police functions. The UN mission would have to monitor and enforce ceasefire and, if necessary, organize discussions or meetings, even if the mediators might be external actors. The mission is the eyes and ears of the international community in the conflict area and as such must constantly monitor the situation and present regular reports to the UN Security Council.

Peacekeeping missions typically have immediate or at best short-term objectives, such as: stop the hostilities: protect the civilian population; demobilize combatants; restore State authority; relaunch democratic governance processes; and organize multiparty elections. Even after the situation has been brought well under control, these objectives circumscribe the mission's capacity to effectively build and consolidate the peace. Once a country is at war, the assumption is for the United Nations to come in, cool down the fires, reinstate established authority, organize and supervise the elections, and then leave after two or three years. The United Nations would have kept the peace, but it might not necessarily have built it. Many have argued that peacebuilding is not within the purview of UN peacekeepers, especially under their present mandates. Yet, unless there are firm guarantees that hostilities have been halted permanently, and the underlying causes of the conflict have been identified and removed, paecekeeping gains could very easily become reversed and ultimately lost.

The Causes of Conflict

Experts have identified three clusters of factors that give rise to conflict: root or structural, proximate and triggers. Structural factors relate to issues of governance and the functioning of State with regard to its relationship with the citizenry, legitimacy, ability to provide basic services and mode of governance. They manifest themselves in weak or overly strong autocratic governments, rampant inequities among the population, corruption, discrimination, extreme poverty and deprivation, human rights deficiencies and a weakened system of adjudication. These cause disaffection among the population, which could eventually lead to uprisings, insurgencies and violent confrontation with established authority.

Proximate factors differ only by degree from structural causes. When discrimination becomes legitimized in the promulgation of laws that target a particular ethnic group, religion or clan, or if there is a precipitous decline in the standard of living, the conditions of conflict become heightened. These factors are one step removed from the triggers of conflict. There are sudden social traumas that spark off hostilities. In Rwanda, for example, there were many elements in the relationship between the Hutus and Tutsis that constituted structural and proximate causes of violence, but it took the shooting down of the presidential aircraft to trigger off the genocide. These factors are further compounded by State weakness, or the status of a shadow or soft State, whose governance capacities are so weak that it can easily be destabilized by internal or external aggressors. It is just one step away from a State failure, invariably resulting from prolonged internal strife, as was the case in Somalia and Liberia.

Stopping the conflict is good, but it is even better to have measures in place to ensure that the situation is not only contained but also improved.

Understanding the causes of conflict is important for post-conflict reconstruction and the maintenance of peace. A typical African country in conflict is poor, with weak government and public institutions, a small private sector, high illiteracy, a narrow skills base and limited capabilities for guaranteeing security. This state of affairs is rendered even more dire by civil strife, whose effects on the economy and the society at large are debilitating. The situation after the conflict is one of destruction: infrastructure destroyed; basic services, water and fuel supplies, and electricity disrupted or lost; and transportation systems barely functioning. Many professional and skilled personnel would very likely have left the country, thus severely circumscribing the ability of institutions to function.

The Consequences of Conflict

In such a post-conflict situation, economic management capacities are seriously weakened, and security cannot be adequately provided. Even where the structures and institutions of democracy do exist, they are usually weak and unable to sustain the workings of a democratic system. Children are out of school, unemployment is very high and a large proportion of the population displaced. The non-physical fallout of war is even more devastating. A large number of people suffer from post-traumatic stress disorder, many women are raped and children traumatized, and abuse among young people would be a serious social problem. The feeling of despondency, bitterness and anger is pervasive, creating the very conditions for a flare up of violence and hostilities.

What are the requirements for the reconstruction and the building of a lasting peace? First is the restoration of established authority throughout the territory.

Stopping the conflict is good, but it is even better to have measures in place to ensure that the situation is not only contained but also improved. It is important to institute programmes and mechanisms that would inevitably address the outcome of the conflict and its antecedents to ensure that there is no sliding back into conflict. In this, the UN peace missions in Africa have suffered their greatest weakness. By giving too much prominence to security responsibilities that need a military predominance in UN peace operations, the requirements for reconstruction, rehabilitation and relaunching of democratic and economic development processes are downplayed and become unresponsive to the need for recovery and the functioning of basic infrastructure and government services. The UN missions in Namibia and Mozambique came closest to full-blown peacebuilding missions, but the requirements for building the peace in general do not feature prominently in the mandates, composition and structure of UN peace missions in Africa. Because of this shortcoming, successful peacekeeping operations have had their gains wiped out by a hasty withdrawal from the post-conflict country before these issues were addressed, as was the case in Somalia, Central African Republic and Liberia, where hostilities resumed shortly after the closure of the peacekeeping operations.

The Elements of Lasting Peace

What are the requirements for the reconstruction and the building of lasting peace? First is the restoration of established authority throughout the territory. After the cessation of hostilities in Sierra Leone, State authority did not extend to more than 10 per cent of the entire territory; the rest was in the hands of the rebels. The UN mission, as its topmost priority, set to help the Government regain control of the country. Second is to sequester and demobilize the insurgents. In a situation where thousands of heavily armed men roam the countryside and wreak havoc among the civilian population with virtually no central authority to control them, it is urgent to have these elements disarmed, demobilized and reintegrated into civilian life. In 1997, Liberia's disarmament and demobilization programme was deeply flawed and half-heartedly undertaken, which led to the holding of a hasty presidential election at which the warlord Charles Taylor intimidated the electorate. It also led the country into another conflict and resulted in complete State failure. By contrast, Sierra Leone's post-conflict activities were very well handled. Combatants were first sequestered, then demobilized and disarmed, and were paid to turn in and destroy their weapons, and camped for eventual reintegration into their respective communities.

Then there is the necessity to relaunch economic activity. The immediate need would be for essential services, such as water, electricity, telecommunications and transportation, to be reinstated. The Government invariably would not have the wherewithal to undertake these activities, having become virtually bankrupt due to State collapse; therefore, the United Nations and the donor community would have to step in and provide the assistance required. Both public and private institutions, which are vital for the resuscitation of the economy, would have to be revived. The fourth requirement is to revive the civil service, which in most cases would have been decimated. The judiciary, in particular, should be reinvigorated early on to bolster the observance of the rule of law, protect human rights and help support security within the country. Programmes should be put in place to bring back and reinstate civil servants who were displaced or in exile.

The United Nations should go beyond the immediacy of the political requirements for consolidating peace and address the broader dimensions of governance.

There is also the need for security reform. In situations of prolonged conflict, security services take on a new culture and entrenched behaviours conditioned by the conflict. It is important to change those behaviours very early on and restructure the army, police and other security and law-enforcement institutions to meet the peacetime needs of the country. Failure to do so could lead to problems, such as those faced by Guinea-Bissau, where security services are still locked in a wartime mentality and have become a liability and an impediment in the democratic process. Not least important is the need for full engagement of the international community to provide assistance for reconstruction and keep the peacebuilding process firmly on course.

Funds Are Difficult to Secure

Three conditions always prevail in post-conflict situations. First, there would be a severe paucity of funds to allow the Government to meet its external obligations and its responsibilities to its people. Second, donors are unwilling to entrust their monies to a government that has lost its capacity for economic and financial management. To compound matters, government corruption is usually very high in post-conflict countries, making it more difficult to attract official development assistance. This has been the experience in Guinea-Bissau and Liberia, as well as in Sierra Leone, where the Government had to set up an anti-corruption commission to address the problem and reassure donors. The third condition concerns the country's relations with the Bretton Woods institutions, particularly the International Monetary Fund (IMF). [The IMF is an organization of nations that was established at a 1944 conference in Bretton Woods, New Hampshire. It works to maintain a stable world financial system and reduce world poverty, and is a major source of assistance to nations with financial difficulties.] A country that has defaulted on its loan repayments would be placed under prescribed sanctions and therefore would not be eligible for further loans. Because the IMF programme would have been suspended, donors would be reluctant to engage directly with this country. This situation makes it more difficult for countries emerging from conflict to keep their reconstruction and peacebuilding efforts on an even keel.

Capacity Building

To ensure that peacekeeping dovetails into peacebuilding and consolidation, the United Nations should go beyond the immediacy of the political requirements for consolidating peace and address the broader dimensions of governance. It would do well to include a robust capacity-building element into its peacebuilding operations in order to help countries emerging from conflict to be invested with good governance and effective public sector management capabilities. This calls for an extensive UN-supported technical assistance programme to plug the skills gaps in key government sectors, as well as a well-focused training programme for public officials. Timor Leste's experience could serve as an ideal model here.

An inter-agency programme needs to be mounted to support the peacebuilding process, with clearly defined roles and responsibilities for each participating agency. Job creation is a priority because economies of post-conflict countries are typically depressed and unemployment is extremely high. Public works employment generation projects are greatly recommended as they provide livelihood to poor households, rehabilitate infrastructure and contribute to reviving domestic demand, which help to stimulate the growth of the local economy. There is also a need to strengthen government structures and institutions to increase synergies between the executive, the judiciary and the legislature. A special programme to bring back skilled workers who left the country is required to fill the gaps and provide services, as was successfully done in Timor Leste.

Reforming the World Bank and IMF

The United Nations should assist countries in organizing donor conferences and prepare Poverty Reduction Strategy Papers, which are the programme contexts for assistance from the Bretton Woods institutions. Countries emerging from conflict would have a set of developmental priorities and be assisted in articulating these needs. The Bretton Woods institutions could be encouraged to create a special facility for these countries. The World Bank has such a facility, but the terms for accessing it are so stringent that most countries that qualify would unlikely benefit much from it. [The World Bank is another organization established at the 1944 Bretton Woods conference that provides financial assistance to nations in need.] The facility must be designed to ensure that the lack of funds does not impede the implementation of basic stabilization programmes, such as starting off the school system, and will operate, if necessary, on a highly concessional or a full-grant basis. IMF regulations are more stringent and do not leave much room for countries to manoeuvre—a situation that has to be reviewed further, because good relations with the Fund are always an important pre-condition for good relations with donors. In all cases, there is a need for a bridging arrangement upon the cessation of hostilities, through which an emergency programme of assistance will be launched to allow the Government to discharge its most basic responsibilities. This programme would target issues, such as emergency food needs, resettlement of the displaced, reintegration of ex-combatants and rehabilitation of child soldiers, for which the United Nations would have to secure the resources needed.

Change Is Already Underway at the UN

The United Nations is in the process of reappraising its role in the prevention of conflict and the maintenance of peace. It has decided to position itself to better respond to the increasing urgency to be more proactive in its peacebuilding activities. In 2000, the General Assembly adopted resolution 55/217 on the causes of conflict and the promotion of durable peace and sustainable development in Africa. In 2001, the [UN] Economic and Social Council issued a Ministerial Declaration, addressing the United Nations role in support of the efforts of African countries to achieve sustainable development.

In 2002, the Council decided to set up ad hoc advisory groups, whose terms of reference were to assess the humanitarian and economic needs of countries emerging from conflict and elaborate a long-term support strategy that would ensure an easy crossover from relief to development. The first such group was set up for Guinea-Bissau in 2002, followed for Burundi in 2003. So far, these groups have proven to be effective mechanisms, have been flexible and efficient, and have brought some synergy among the partners in support of their respective countries. They have played an important advocacy role on behalf of their client countries and have guided Governments, encouraging them to embark on courses of action that would get the backing of and assistance from donors.

But perhaps a more formal response to the need is yet to come. Secretary-General Kofi Annan in 2004 created the High-Level Panel on Threats, Challenges and Change, whose report has a number of recommendations for the creation of a Peacebuilding Commission, which was considered by Heads of State and Government at the 2005 World Summit. With this decision, peacebuilding is formally granted a place within the structure, functions and mandates of the United Nations. A peacebuilding support office would be established to serve as the secretariat to the Commission and enable the Secretary-General to easily integrate system-wide peacebuilding policies and strategies, develop best practices and provide cohesive support and leadership in field operations. On 20 December 2005, the General Assembly, acting concurrently with the Security Council, decided to establish the Peacebuilding Commission. In our bid to render the United Nations more relevant to present-day needs and realities, strengthening its capabilities to build and consolidate the peace is one measure that would close the door on one threat to peace and security in a cost-effective and positive way.

6

UN Peacekeepers Have Harmed Those They Are Supposed to Protect

William P. Hoar

William P. Hoar is a frequent contributor to the New American, *a publication of the John Birch Society.*

UN peacekeepers, charged with providing relief and restoring calm to nations torn by conflict, have often been guilty of creating a predatory sexual culture in the places they are sent to protect. In numerous instances, they have been accused of rape, forced prostitution, and pedophilia. Yet because of the sovereignty of nations contributing forces to UN peacekeeping missions, it has proven difficult to discipline those who have committed such crimes. The UN cannot be trusted with the kind of power that would be necessary for it to function effectively as a peacekeeper in the world.

Item: The United Nations' [UN] official website asks the question, "What is peacekeeping?" then answers in part as follows: "Peacekeeping is a way to help countries torn by conflict create conditions for sustainable peace. U.N. peacekeepers—soldiers and military officers, civilian police officers and civilian personnel from many countries—monitor and observe peace processes that emerge in post-conflict situations and assist ex-combatants to implement the peace agreements they have signed. Such assistance comes in many forms in-

William P. Hoar, "Who Will Keep Us Safe from the Peacekeepers?" *The New American*, vol. 21, July 11, 2005, pp. 38–39. Copyright © 2005 American Opinion Publishing Incorporated. Reproduced by permission.

cluding confidence-building measures, power-sharing arrangements, electoral support, strengthening the rule of law, and economic and social development."

Correction: The activities of UN peacekeepers do come in many forms—unfortunately, these often include rape, forced prostitution, pedophilia, and other sexual abuses, all of which have been recently brought to light among UN troops in the Democratic Republic of Congo, involving girls as young as 11. After media exposés of the lurid practices, the UN was forced to initiate its own investigation—though it took another six months before its results were released.

The United Nations has tolerated such behavior for years, say human-rights groups. According to a Danish film documentary, for example, UN troops had a large hand in spreading the AIDS virus in Cambodia in the early 1990s, with peacekeepers having sex with locals—children and prostitutes. Asked for his reaction, a UN official shown in the film answers, "Boys will be boys."

One UN publication, *Africa Renewal,* noted in April of 2005: "As recently as 2002 allegations surfaced that UN personnel and humanitarian workers at UN-administered camps in Liberia, Sierra Leone and Guinea were forcing refugee women and young children to provide sexual favours in exchange for desperately needed food, medicines and other relief supplies." Those reports are "strikingly similar to those made in the DRC [Democratic Republic of Congo]" this past year.

The Congo scandal, it seems certain, is just the tip of the proverbial iceberg. At least one senior UN official involved in the Bunia refugee camp in the DRC has been implicated in the sexual abuse, according to published accounts—which also have noted that after the scandal broke, investigators were threatened with retaliation by peacekeepers. The *Times of London* reported about Russian pilots among the peacekeepers, who "paid young girls with jars of mayonnaise and jam to have sex with them. They filmed the sessions and sent the tapes to Russia. But the men were tipped off and left the area before U.N. investigators arrived."

The Problem Is Widespread

The Congo outrage is "the latest in a string of scandals that have hit U.N. peacekeeping operations around the world," testified Dr. Nile Gardiner, a fellow in Anglo-American Security Policy at the Heritage Foundation, before the House Subcommittee on Africa, Global Human Rights and International Operations on March 1 [2005]. "Indeed, it appears that U.N. peacekeeping missions frequently create a predatory sexual culture, with refugees the victims of U.N. staff who demand sexual favors in exchange for food, and U.N. troops who rape women at gunpoint. Allegations of sexual abuse stretch back at least a decade, to operations in Kosovo, Sierra Leone, Liberia, and Guinea. Despite previous U.N. investigations—and Kofi Annan's declaration of a policy of 'zero tolerance' toward such conduct—little appears to have changed in the field."

There are some 80,000 peacekeeping troops from about 100 nations in 17 countries, a number that keeps rising. American taxpayers foot the largest portion of the total peacekeeping bill, around 27 percent (the share is higher in the Congo mission). Between 2001 and 2005, U.S. contributions to such peacekeeping operations have amounted to some $3.6 billion.

Astonishingly, UN officials have complained that, because nations want to protect their sovereignty, the world body can do little to discipline such abusive peacekeepers. We are supposed to believe that if we only gave more power to the world army, there would be less abuse of those the peacekeepers are supposed to be protecting. The chief of staff for Secretary-General Kofi Annan told a U.S. congressional panel that, "for me, the United Nations is not over-sized, over-resourced or under-supervised by its member states." He complained of too much supervision, saying the secretary-general is "mired in a web of governmental committees and outdated rules that impede his freedom to manage."

This is not just a matter of a few bad apples abusing their power. A liberal reporter for the *Washington Post*, Keith Richburg, had his eyes opened when he covered a number of UN operations in Africa; several are described in his compelling book *Out of America: A Black Man Confronts Africa*. For example, he says that events in Somalia dashed the hopes of the world, as well as his own, "that Africa might somehow become the testing ground of the New World Order and the idea of benign military intervention."

Testing the New World Order

Richburg describes the horrendous bureaucratic hurdles imposed by the UN in Somalia. He also recalls journalists and international do-gooders partying in formal evening wear, with rock bands blaring, at a benefit banquet—while Somali children and refugees "climbed trees or onto nearby walls just for a glimpse of what must have seemed a very weird foreign tribal ritual." As for the warring parties, the UN just threw money at them, which is rightly called extortion by the author. The UN "was effectively paying the thugs not to shoot the [peacekeeping] soldiers coming in to keep the peace." Moreover, it didn't work.

Elsewhere, he recounts the horrendous brutality in Rwanda, where the UN was complicit in mass murder. In one incident, Prime Minister Agathe Uwilingiyimana tried to find refuge at the UN compound but was found by her killers, dragged to the street, and executed. That was about the time, Richburg writes, "when ten Belgian troops arrived to protect her. Following an instruction radioed from the UN headquarters in Kigali, the Belgians laid down their arms, hoping to avoid a confrontation with the crowd; they too were brutally tortured and executed."

Such disgraces took place while the UN was supposedly calling the shots. Do we really want to make the military arm of such a world body more "effective"?

The UN's record when it has the upper hand over vulnerable populations is hardly reassuring. Strangely, it is often those who complain the loudest about the occasional unlawful actions of U.S. troops—who are governed by a system of checks and balances and operate under a bona fide military justice system, unlike UN troops—who would empower foreign troops with more power, even over American citizens and soldiers. Yet, as the Romans asked centuries ago, who will guard us from the guardians? A government big enough to enforce world peace is big enough to impose world tyranny.

Indeed, if the UN had enough power to enforce what it calls global peace—meaning a lack of resistance to its dictates—it surely would tyrannize the world.

7

Despite Failures, the United Nations Plays an Important Global Role

Mark Turner

Mark Turner covers the United Nations for the Financial Times.

A host of serious international crises have returned the United Nations to the center of the world stage. In 2005 the United Nations appeared to be losing the confidence of the world. A year later, it seems overwhelmed with the magnitude of the work, without adequate resources to fully respond. Many feel that the United Nations does important work despite its flaws.

One year ago [2005] the United Nations [UN] was in turmoil, reeling from a wave of scandals, hamstrung by disagreements over terrorism, human rights and nuclear proliferation, and caught in an acrimonious and unravelling reform process.

Some asked whether they even might be witnessing the death throes of the 60-year-old organisation, as its creaking architecture struggled to respond to the new challenges.

Yet today, as a panoply of leaders assemble to address this week's General Assembly session, the UN is back at the centre of almost every major dispute on the planet.

Despite divisions among its members, the Security Council is tackling crises from Lebanon to Iran, from North Korea to Darfur and the Palestinian territories, let alone a wealth of lesser crises in Africa, Haiti and East Timor.

And notwithstanding its differences, the council has, or is at least trying to craft, joint positions on nearly all of them—albeit often with limited results, such as in Darfur.

The United Nations Is Active Around the World

The US administration, public pronouncements aside, is embracing the UN in a way few would have imagined a year ago. By dispatching troops to Lebanon, Europe has put itself back in the business of peacekeeping.

The Security Council adopted a resolution threatening sanctions on Iran. Asia broke with precedent and allowed the UN to take a strong stand over North Korea's missile tests. The Middle East welcomed [UN secretary-general] Kofi Annan's mediation on Lebanon and now wants the council to take centre stage on the wider peace process.

As the mandates have mounted, the UN's operational arms have seen unprecedented growth. Were the proposed Darfur mission to proceed, the UN would have more than 100,000 peacekeepers under its command in close to 20 countries: a huge challenge. Its aid agencies, financed by a new standing fund, are active in many more.

The UN is running a criminal investigation into the assassination of Lebanon's former prime minister [Rafik al-Hariri] and is conducting elections in the Congo. It handled the transfer of Liberia's former dictator [Charles Taylor] to an international court, and is co-ordinating the worldwide response to avian flu.

Stretched Thinly

In fact, in stark contrast to last year, UN officials' main fear is no longer in being sidelined but in being asked to do too much, too fast, without adequate tools to do so. "Our new challenge today is in the ricochet of world opinion," says Robert Orr, an adviser to Mr Annan. "Everyone is turning to us but we have the same capacity as yesterday."

Some analysts are asking whether the UN might be facing a new "early-90s" moment, when euphoria over the end of the cold war led to an exponential growth in its missions, followed by a string of catastrophes when they were overwhelmed.

But the atmospherics in 2006 are not the same. Rather than proclaiming the dawn of a new era, diplomats say the world is coming back to the UN, faults and all, because the challenges are so difficult that there is no one left to turn to.

The UN Secretariat, chastened by the disasters of Bosnia and Rwanda, and mismanagement of the oil-for-food programme, has since then become more realistic about what is achievable with what resources.

But, as one official suggested, while "the UN has, the member states have not".

UN appeals for more flexibility in hiring staff and allocating resources to manage its mandates were all but rejected by the developing world.

8

Member Nations Must Provide Resources the UN Needs for Its Mission

Ann Florini

Ann Florini is senior fellow at the Brookings Institution.

Member nations do not provide the UN with the quality of attention and support that is necessary for the organization to function effectively. As a result, the United Nations is mired in serious structural, economic, and cultural difficulties.

When fifty-one nations signed the United Nations [UN] Charter in San Francisco ... [in 1945] they aimed to save the world from the global catastrophes they had endured twice in three decades—major wars between countries. But history has a way of confounding the best-laid plans. As the Cold War and decolonization transformed the world, the UN morphed into a body of 191 member countries with responsibilities ranging from feeding the hungry to protecting the innocent from the ravages of civil wars—responsibilities it is not designed to meet.

From its beginnings, the UN has at best muddled through. Yet its responsibilities continue to grow, as governments look for a handy place to dump global problems. Its peace and security function now has the UN struggling to manage more than 70,000 troops and civilians drawn from 103 countries, deployed in eighteen missions in some of the world's most desperate conflicts: Congo, Liberia, Haiti, Sudan. The UN deals with over 19 million people displaced from their homes by violence or natural disaster. It oversees global efforts to help millions of tsunami victims, and toils to call the world's attention to some twenty "forgotten emergencies" that threaten millions more. And as the United States has recently rediscovered, the UN remains a powerful source of international legitimacy and a vital diplomatic instrument for national governments.

But all this activity depends on a fundamentally unsound institutional base. The UN's fifteen-country Security Council, the only UN body with teeth, gives lopsided power to the victors of World War II. The General Assembly, where all 191 nations theoretically have equal voice, has degenerated into a sclerotic mess of largely pointless debates on a mind-numbing agenda covering every conceivable issue. The fifty-three-member Economic and Social Council is essentially worthless. The Secretariat suffers from a deadwood-ridden staff, extreme micro-management by member states, and an inadequate oversight system that allows plenty of waste, fraud, and abuse.

Turnaround Plan

In response to the UN's evident shortcomings, Secretary General Kofi Annan called upon the members to make 2005 the year of the UN's renaissance. Annan had in mind a grand bargain. The world's rich and powerful would take seriously poor countries' concerns with economic development and would relax their stranglehold on the Security Council. The developing world would take seriously concerns with terrorism, human rights, [nuclear] non-proliferation, and the need for drastic changes in the organization's dysfunctional management structures. That grand bargain was to be adopted at the 2005 UN Summit in September, the largest gathering ever of national leaders.

But the grand bargain collapsed into the politicking and short-sightedness that have long plagued efforts at UN reform. Instead of a long stride forward into the new century, the Summit achieved only baby steps: dissolution of the utterly discredited Human Rights Commission; establishment of a Peacebuilding Commission to create a much-needed central coordinator for post-war reconstruction; and—surprisingly—agreement that governments who fail to meet their "responsibility to protect" their citizens from such basic threats as genocide risk surrendering their cherished sovereignty to an international community that may choose to act on behalf of those citizens.

The member countries have never invested the financial and human resources needed to make the UN work well.

Having missed one golden opportunity to revitalize the flawed but still essential United Nations, the world now must figure out how to do better. Step one is to assign responsibility where it belongs: overwhelmingly with the member countries. Blaming "the UN" (usually meaning the Secretariat) for all the scandals and failures is like blaming the Kennedy Center if the National Symphony Orchestra has an off night. While there is an institutional responsibility to make sure the roof isn't leaking and the ticket-sellers aren't pocketing the proceeds, it's the musicians who have to perform. At the UN, the players are prone to breaking into fistfights at concert time—if they show up at all.

Putting the Blame Where It Belongs

The member countries have never invested the financial and human resources needed to make the UN work well. Many act like absentee landlords, pocketing rents in the form of cushy jobs for a handful of their nationals but otherwise largely ignoring the institution. A few hard-core opponents of reform—

insiders point to Syria, Pakistan, Venezuela, Cuba, Egypt, and Iran—actively subvert attempts to make the UN function efficiently and effectively. The U.S., where Congress goes into periodic fits of rage over revelations of misdeeds such as the oil-for-food scandal, has only fitfully invested in the long-term, patient diplomacy needed to build consensus for meaningful change, and has sometimes shot itself in the foot with bullying tactics like withholding of dues.

The small reforms agreed upon to date may still prove the spark for a real UN renaissance—if a whole lot of people act quickly. Annan must both press forward with internal reforms already underway and propose new steps to the General Assembly before it votes in December on the budget for the next two years. The highly respected president of this year's General Assembly, Swedish ambassador Jan Eliasson, faces an uphill but essential battle to fundamentally change the workings of the dysfunctional Assembly. U.S. Ambassador John Bolton must engage effectively but, given the realities of anti-Americanism, quietly with pro-reform forces in New York, use his great influence with Congress to ensure it supports a productive reform agenda, and prod the Bush Administration to engage governments around the world in the UN reform process. And the member states need to regain control of their own delegations in New York, who too often serve personal interests at the expense of national ones.

If all this is done, the UN may be reborn. If not, the UN will hobble into an arthritic old age. And there are no vigorous young replacements in sight.

9

The International Community Needs the Human Rights Council

Jorge Taiana

Jorge Taiana is foreign affairs minister of Argentina.

The new United Nations Human Rights Council (HRC) was formed to guarantee enforcement of human rights around the world. In order to correct human rights abuses of the past, such as those that occurred in Argentina, it will be guided by important values, including universality, objectivity, and constructive international dialogue, in the defense of fundamental human rights.

On May 9 [2006], the Argentine Republic was elected by the United Nations [UN] General Assembly to integrate the Human Rights Council, the new U.N. body that will replace the Commission on Human Rights established in 1947.

Our country was elected by the United Nations General Assembly as one of the 47 member states to this new Council. We are grateful to all those states that, bearing in mind our tragic history of gross and systematic human-rights violations, valued our present record and commitments in this field. This election implies a deep responsibility toward all persons, organizations and governments that expect this body to guarantee a major enforcement of human rights around the world.

This new body will be permanent and directly subsidiary to the General Assembly, which will enable it to deeply ana-

Jorge Taiana, "Universal Human-Rights Protection," *The Washington Times*, May 21, 2006, p. B03. Copyright © 2006 News World Communications, Inc. Reproduced by permission of the publisher and author.

lyze human-rights violations in any and all countries. The council work shall be guided by the principles of universality, impartiality, objectivity, non-selectivity and constructive international dialogue. It shall have to report in time to all bodies and agencies that, like the Security Council, may prevent or stop gross and systematic violations.

This new council must transcend incidental political debates and become a stable, central and permanent element of international relations. In the past, the Argentine society suffered the politicization and selectivity of the U.N. Commission on Human Rights, which privileged the bipolar balance of power at that time instead of defense of fundamental and permanent human rights, such as the right to life.

Despite thousands of reports received at the commission during the last military dictatorship (1976–1983), my country's government was never condemned, and the indifference of the majority of U.N. member states forced creation of a special working group to publicly expose the gross and systematic violations in Argentina.

The Human Rights Council offers the international community the opportunity to guarantee an efficient and effective international protection system.

We have learned from our own history, and since the return to democracy have assumed a position based on principles in the defense and promotion of human rights. We have ratified the great majority of the regional and universal treaties on human rights. And, as very few countries in the world, we have granted constitutional hierarchy to these human-rights instruments. Argentina permanently cooperates with international monitoring bodies and participates in every forum with the goal of improving existing standards in this field worldwide.

Since the beginning of debate on reforming the U.N. system, [Argentine] President Nestor Kirchner's government has strongly supported strengthening human rights within the U.N. to put this on the same footing as other relevant issues, such as developing and maintaining peace and international security.

This is not just a choice but an obligation for all states in light of the importance human rights have today for peace, development and democratic stability.

We must highlight and reinforce the true importance of the commission's contribution to developing international human-rights law over several decades by developing standards and treaties. At this first stage of the council, we must ensure procedural matters do not displace substantive issues and obtain prompt approval of the International Convention for the Protection of all Persons from Forced Disappearances, as well as the Declaration on the Rights of Indigenous Peoples.

The Human Rights Council offers the international community the opportunity to guarantee an efficient and effective international protection system. This is an obligation of all states that have assumed the responsibility to be a part of this early stage, always remembering that respect for the principle of negotiation must not imply negotiation of principles.

Thirty years after the military coup that disrupted the institutions and the fundamental rights of the people of my country, Argentina commits itself to making a sound contribution so the U.N. Human Rights Council may meet the demands of the 21st century on this issue, which is essential for the survival of our nations.

10

Human Rights Abusers Are Serving on the UN Human Rights Council

Brett D. Schaefer

Brett D. Schaefer is Jay Kingham fellow in international regulatory affairs in the Margaret Thatcher Center for Freedom, a division of the Kathryn and Shelby Cullom Davis Institute for International Studies at the Heritage Foundation.

The new UN Human Rights Council was formed to replace the discredited UN Commission on Human Rights. However, the Human Rights Council is vulnerable to the same corrupting factors as was the Commission on Human Rights. A lack of rigorous membership standards has resulted in several known human rights abusers holding positions on the Human Rights Council. The United States should hold the Human Rights Council to a high standard of accountability, and withhold future financial support and participation until it is clear that the standard is met.

The 2005 World Summit Outcome Document's agreement to replace the discredited Commission on Human Rights was a historic opportunity to replace the United Nations' [UN] premier human rights body with a strong advocate for human rights. But negotiations in the General Assembly seriously weakened the reform proposals and resulted in modest change and not fundamental reform. Rather than adopt strong

Brett D. Schaefer, "Human Rights Relativism Redux: U.N. Human Rights Council Mirrors Discredited Human Rights Commission," www.heritage.org, May 10, 2006, Web Memo #1069. Copyright © 2006 The Heritage Foundation. Reproduced by permission.

criteria to prevent human rights abusers from sitting on the new Council, the resolution merely requires member states to "take into account" a candidate's human rights record when they vote for HRC [Human Rights Council] members. Worse, the resolution set a higher bar to suspend an elected HRC member—a vote of two-thirds of the General Assembly—than the simple majority necessary to win a seat.

U.S. Concerns

The new Council's lack of membership criteria leave it open to infiltration and manipulation by the world's worst human rights abusers. This led the U.S. to vote against the HRC in the General Assembly. "Absent stronger mechanisms for maintaining credible membership, the United States could not join consensus on this resolution," explained U.S. Ambassador to the UN, John Bolton. "We did not have sufficient confidence in this text to be able to say that the HRC would be better than its predecessor." The U.S. was joined in its opposition only by Israel, the Marshall Islands, and Palau. Significantly, Burma, Syria, Libya, China, Cuba, Ethiopia, Sudan, Saudi Arabia, and Zimbabwe all voted in favor of the new Council.

Despite promises by a number of nations to vote against human rights abusers and a series of public pledges by candidates to uphold human rights, the U.S. remained concerned that human rights abusers would gain HRC membership, and so it pledged to "actively campaign on behalf of candidates genuinely committed to the promotion and protection of human rights [and] actively campaign against states that systematically abuse human rights" [U.S. Department of State, 2006]. The Administration also announced that it would not run for a seat on the HRC in 2006 but might in 2007 if the Council proves effective.

Human Rights Abusers on the New Council

The early signs have not been positive. Only half of the candidates in the May 9 [2006] election are considered "free" by

Freedom House. Nearly 20 percent of the 66 candidates are considered "not free" by Freedom House, including notable human rights abusers Algeria, Cuba, China, Iran, Pakistan, Saudi Arabia, and Russia. Several of these countries were listed in Freedom House's "The Worst of the Worst: The World's Most Repressive Societies 2005." While countries like Sudan and Zimbabwe chose not to run for election, nothing prevents them from running in the future. They could follow the lead of several countries this time around that made pledges of their commitment to human rights that fly in the face of their track records:

• The Chinese government pledged that it is "committed to the promotion and protection of human rights and fundamental freedoms of the Chinese People. . . . The National People's Congress has adopted nearly 300 laws and regulations related to the protection of civil and political rights, ensuring complete freedom of the Chinese people in movement, employment, access to information, religious belief and ways of life."

• Cuba claims that "Cuban women and men have achieved significant progress in enjoinment of all their human rights. Either in the area of civil and political rights . . . the Cuban people can show to the world, with deep modesty, but with full satisfaction and pride, its tremendous achievements."

• In its pledge, Pakistan notes, "Promotion of human dignity, fundamental freedoms and human rights, equal status and rights of the followers of all religions and prohibition of discrimination on account of religion, race, caste or creed etc are enshrined in Articles 9-29 of the Constitution. . . . Sustainable democracy and empowerment at grass root level, through good governance, have been established at the local, provincial and national levels. . . ."

• Saudi Arabia claims a "confirmed commitment with the defense, protection and promotion of human rights. . . .

Saudi Arabia pursues the policy of active cooperation with international organizations in the field of Human Rights and fundamental freedoms."

The May 9 election validated U.S. concerns. When the dust settled, it was clear that simply creating a new Council would not convince the General Assembly to spurn the candidacies of human rights abusers. Despite their poor human rights records and the transparently disingenuous nature of their pledges, China, Cuba, Pakistan, and Saudi Arabia all succeeded in gaining support from a majority of the General Assembly, thus winning seats on the Council. They were joined by fellow abusers and unfree governments in Algeria and Russia.

Congress should tie future funding for the HRC to the body's effectiveness.

These countries were key players in undermining the effectiveness of the now-defunct Commission on Human Rights, and so it is very likely that they will play the same role on the Council, steering it away from confronting human rights abuses within their borders and in general. The United States must carefully monitor the performance of the Council and use its influence to ensure that this does not occur.

Scrutinizing the Human Rights Council

As John Bolton explained, "The real test [of the HRC] will be the quality of membership that emerges on this Council and whether it takes effective action to address serious human rights abuse cases like Sudan, Cuba, Iran, Zimbabwe, Belarus, and Burma." The election of human rights abusers like Algeria, China, Cuba, Pakistan, Russia, and Saudi Arabia demonstrates the failure of the UN of this first test of the HRC.

The question remains, however, whether these countries will dominate the new Council. The ease with which these countries were elected demonstrates that human rights abusers can and do wield great influence. The U.S. should work with other nations to ensure that new HRC members—Algeria, China, Cuba, Pakistan, Russia, and Saudi Arabia—be the first targets of the Council's periodic human rights reviews. The quality of these reviews will be a useful tool to measure the dedication, effectiveness, and willingness of the HRC to confront human rights abusers and to resist the influence of those most determined to undermine its work. Only if the HRC conducts strong, condemnatory reviews of these well-known abusers should the U.S. consider seeking a seat in the future.

To increase chances that the Council will be effective and prevent U.S. taxpayer funds from going to waste, Congress should tie future funding for the HRC to the body's effectiveness. Although the [George W.] Bush Administration has promised to fund the HRC during the current year, Congress should consider its performance when debating appropriations for the United Nations in the coming months. Congress also should request that the State Department report on the Council's performance and restrict funds if the Council fails to confront prominent human rights abusers, such as China, Cuba, Sudan, and Zimbabwe.

11

The UN Population Fund Helps China Persecute Women and Kill Children

National Right to Life News

National Right to Life News *is a publication of National Right to Life. National Right to Life is a U.S. organization that opposes abortion, which it considers to be the murder of an unborn child.*

Numerous credible sources, including Amnesty International, have reported that the United Nations Population Fund (UNFPA) has provided financial and technical support for China's repressive one-child-per-couple policy, which coerces women and families to have abortions. The United States is right to refuse funding for the UNFPA, which is guilty of crimes against humanity.

Like the Good Samaritan, she picked up a newborn baby girl who had been abandoned on the side of the road and took her home. Even though she was pregnant with her first child, she could not bring herself to turn her back on this innocent and helpless infant. Then the knock came on her door. The decision had been made; Chinese law only allowed her to have one child and since she had taken a baby girl into her protection she would be required to abort the child in her womb. In China the terrible consequence for her compassionate act was that her unborn child was killed through a forced abortion.

This heart-wrenching story, told by the victim during a congressional hearing, is all too common in China. For the last two decades the United Nations Population Fund, with the misfitting acronym UNFPA, has shockingly defended the coercive Chinese population control program. Thankfully, President George [W.] Bush has once again put the United States solidly on the side of the victims and against the oppressors by refusing to fund UNFPA.

Women Testify About Their Experiences

The victims have told me their horrific stories about the Chinese one-child-per-couple policy. At one religious freedom meeting in China, I asked what the participants knew about forced abortion policies. All three women in the group broke down in tears as they shared with me how they all had been forced to have abortions. One woman talked about how she thought God was going to protect her baby, but she was not able to escape the abortion.

Other women who have gained asylum in the United States because of China's coercive population control program have told me terrible stories of crippling fines, imprisonment of family members, and destruction of homes and property—all to force abortion and sterilization upon millions of women. According to the most recent State Department Human Rights Report, one consequence of "the country's birth limitation policies" is that 56% of the world's female suicides occur in China, which is five times the world average and approximately 500 suicides by women per day.

Since 1979, UNFPA has been the chief apologist and cheerleader for China's coercive one-child-per-couple policy.

Mrs. Gao Xiao Duan, a former administrator of a Chinese Planned Birth Control Office, testified before Congress about

China's policies. She explained, "Once I found a woman who was nine months pregnant, but did not have a birth-allowed certificate. According to the policy, she was forced to undergo an abortion surgery. In the operation room I saw how the aborted child's lips were sucking, how its limbs were stretching. A physician injected poison into its skull, and the child died, and it was thrown into the trash can. . . . I was a monster in the daytime, injuring others by the Chinese communist authorities' barbaric planned-birth policy, but in the evening, I was like all other women and mothers, enjoying my life with my children. . . . [T]o all those injured women, to all those children who were killed, I want to repent and say sincerely that I'm sorry!"

While Mrs. Gao acknowledged her part in these human rights atrocities and courageously told her story, UNFPA continues to side with the Chinese government.

Since 1979, UNFPA has been the chief apologist and cheerleader for China's coercive one-child-per-couple policy. Despite numerous credible forced abortion reports from impeccable sources, including human rights organizations like Amnesty International, journalists, former Chinese population control officials, and, above all, from the women victims themselves, high officials at UNFPA always dismiss and explain it all away. UNFPA has funded, provided crucial technical support, and, most importantly, provided cover for massive crimes of forced abortion and involuntary sterilization.

Time and again, high officials of UNFPA have defended the indefensible and called voluntary that which is anything but. The former executive director of UNFPA, Nafis Sadik, said, "China has every reason to feel proud of and pleased with its remarkable achievements made in its family planning policy. The country could offer its experiences and special expertise to help other countries." On CBS *Nightwatch* she said, "The UNFPA firmly believes, and so does the government of the People's Republic of China, that their program is a totally voluntary program." And Sven Burmester, UNFPA's man in Beijing, gushed over China's achievements, "In strictly quantitative terms, it was the most successful family-planning policy ever developed."

The UN Provides Cover for Human Rights Abuses

Make no mistake that China covets UNFPA financial and verbal support of their program as a "Good-Housekeeping seal of approval" to whitewash its human rights violations. I traveled to China and met with the head of its population control program, Peng Peiyun. In our lengthy conversation, Madame Peng Peiyun told me over and over again that there was no coercion in China, and then she cited UNFPA's participation in the program and UNFPA's public statements where UNFPA leaders have defended it. The United States should not help UNFPA cover up China's crimes against women and children.

A 19-year-old law called "the Kemp-Kasten amendment" gives the President authority to disqualify an organization from receiving U.S. funding if that organization "supports or participates in the management of a program of coercive abortion or involuntary sterilization."

Presidents Ronald Reagan and George H.W. Bush used this law to prevent UNFPA from receiving U.S. funding because UNFPA operated in China. President Bush even vetoed the 1989 Foreign Operations Appropriations bill to prevent government funding from going to UNFPA.

When Bill Clinton became president, he unilaterally determined that UNFPA did not violate the law and U.S. funding began to flow to UNFPA. But UNFPA's activities were so egregious that even during one year of the Clinton presidency, Congress successfully withheld all funding from UNFPA.

The George W. Bush Administration reexamined the UNFPA issue in 2001, and through the Department of State determined that UNFPA's activities in China violated Kemp-

Kasten, thereby making them ineligible for U.S. funding. On July 21, 2001, Secretary of State Colin Powell wrote, "Regrettably, the PRC has in place a regime of severe penalties on women who have unapproved births. This regime plainly operates to coerce pregnant women to have abortions in order to avoid the penalties and therefore amounts to a 'program of coercive abortion.'" ". . . UNFPA's support of, and involvement in, China's population-planning activities allows the Chinese government to implement more effectively its program of coercive abortion. Therefore, it is not permissible to continue funding UNFPA at this time." The funds that would have gone to UNFPA were instead given to assist other organizations.

UNFPA remains guilty of shamelessly supporting and whitewashing terrible crimes against humanity, and the United States will have no part in subsidizing them.

After the Bush Administration determined that UNFPA violated the law, three members of the House attempted to change the law so that UNFPA can receive funding even if it continues to support China's program. Reps. Maloney, Crowley, and Lowey have all offered amendments and supported bills to force funding to UNFPA.

But each of those attempts to change human rights law has been defeated. UNFPA and its friends on Capitol Hill continue to make outrageous claims that tens of thousands of women die if other organizations besides UNFPA receive U.S. funding, but their claims are unsubstantiated and illogical, especially since the funding is not cut but is instead given to other organizations.

An Official Policy

In 2002, China explicitly stated its Draconian population control program in law, but UNFPA still continues to support the Chinese program. The Bush Administration has consistently found UNFPA ineligible to receive funding, most recently releasing a July 15, 2004, letter where Secretary Powell said, "China continues to employ coercion in its birth planning program, including through severe penalties for 'out of plan births'. . . . UNFPA continues its support and involvement in China's coercive birth limitation program in counties where China's restrictive law and penalties are enforced by government officials."

UNFPA remains guilty of shamelessly supporting and whitewashing terrible crimes against humanity, and the United States will have no part in subsidizing them. In refusing to fund UNFPA, President Bush has taken the side of the oppressed and has refused to cooperate with the oppressor. UNFPA has aggressively defended a barbaric policy that makes brothers and sisters illegal, and makes women the pawns of the population control cadres.

If UNFPA lobbied the Chinese government to stop forced abortion as aggressively as it lobbies the United States to overturn human rights policy, there would be less suffering in China today.

12

The UN Millennium Development Goals Are Important for Women

Nadia Johnson

Nadia Johnson is the economic and social justice program coordinator of Women's Environment and Development Organization (WEDO).

The United Nations is an important advocate for the rights of women worldwide. The UN Millennium Declaration commits governments to promote gender equality and empowerment, and the Millennium Development Goals that address poverty, education, health and the environment are of particular importance for women. Nevertheless, a large gap remains between promises and implementation. Grassroots advocacy will continue to be necessary, to push the UN to continue addressing the needs of women throughout the world.

When heads of governments from around the world—the overwhelming majority of who[m] are men—met at the United Nations [UN] headquarters in New York in September 2005, women advocates worldwide paid considerable attention. The 2005 World Summit was yet another crucial avenue of engagement for monitoring and advocating implementation of the Beijing Platform for Action, adopted by 189 governments at the 1995 UN Fourth World Conference on Women in China, and other significant international policy agreements won by women in the past decade.

The aim of the 2005 World Summit was to reach consensus on a package of proposals linking peace and security, human rights and development with UN reform. The UN Millennium Development Goals [MDG] (The Millennium Development Goals for 2015), which are aimed at combating poverty and stimulating sustainable development, were a central part of the package.

The UN Millennium Development Goals were issued by the UN Secretary General in 2001 as a "road map" for implementing the Millennium Declaration agreed by 191 governments at the September 2000 UN Millennium Summit.

The Declaration commits governments "to promote gender equality and the empowerment of women as effective ways to combat poverty, hunger and disease and to stimulate development that is truly sustainable." The Declaration also addresses "the equal rights and opportunities of women and men" and pledges "to combat all forms of violence against women and to implement the Convention on the Elimination of All Forms of Discrimination against Women" (CEDAW).

Goal 3 calls for gender equality and women's empowerment, and the MDGS as a whole address several of the 12 Critical Areas of Concern in the Platform for Action adopted at the 1995 Fourth World Conference on Women in Beijing, namely poverty (1), education (2), health (5) and environmental sustainability (7).

The Gap Between Promises and Action

The United Nations has been a galvanizing force for women's advocacy worldwide, facilitating their efforts to define a comprehensive global agenda for peace and human rights, gender equality and women's empowerment and poverty eradication and sustainable development. At the key global conferences and summits of the 1990s ("The Millennium Development Goals for 2015") women participated actively to shape economic, social and political development. In these settings advocates established strategic mechanisms, influenced resolutions and won crucial commitments to set a far-reaching global policy agenda that recognizes gender equality and women's empowerment as essential components of poverty eradication, human development and human rights.

Yet there continues to be a large gap between these promises and implementation at the international and national level, even as the situation of poor women, in particular, worsens dramatically in the face of inaction. The impact of the HIV/AIDS pandemic has further increased women's income-earning, domestic and care-giving responsibilities. The lack of land tenure or inheritance rights and economic trends such as water privatization undermine the ability of women to own, manage, use and conserve natural resources and to provide for themselves and their families. Macroeconomic and national policies keep women concentrated in the informal sector without job or safety protections and in the lowest paying, most hazardous jobs in the formal wage economy, while rendering their unpaid household labor invisible. Women still earn less than men for the same work and remain drastically under-represented in decision-making.

To a certain extent the hard work paid off—advocates did archive some significant gains on gender equality.

Women's Input Is Essential

In the MDG drafting process WEDO [Women's Environment and Development Organization] and other women's rights advocates argued that gender equality and women's empowerment are essential cross-cutting components for achievement of all the goals, be it poverty eradication, protecting the environment or access to health care. Nonetheless, advocates felt, the MDGS do contain time-bound targets for holding governments and international institutions accountable; and they are mutually reinforcing—progress towards one goal affects progress towards the others.

Moreover, the MDG 2015 deadline has had the broad support of the 191 UN member states, UN agencies and international trade and financial institutions. It would be the focus of the review and follow up processes to important UN conferences and summits providing further opportunities to push for gender sensitivity across all the goals, to demand adequate resources and equitable global economic policies consistent with social and environmental needs and to link the MDGS to other ongoing global and national policy processes.

Outcomes of the 2005 World Summit

In the months leading up to the Summit, advocates in every region highlighted what was at stake for women in a list of demands to government—gender equality and women's empowerment, a greater focus on human security, conflict prevention and the equal participation of women in decision-making on peace and security issues and for a shift from market-based decision-making to a human rights-based approach to policy and planning.

To a certain extent the hard work paid off—advocates did achieve some significant gains on gender equality. The MDG on women's empowerment and gender equality has been expanded from an original focus on primary education to include pledges to end impunity [lack of consequences] for violence against women, ensure universal access to reproductive health and the right to own and inherit property, provide equal access to labor protections and increase representation of women in government decision-making bodies. Also positive for women were promises to implement Security Council Resolution 1325, which promotes women's increased participation in peace and security processes, and to protect populations from genocide, war crimes, ethnic cleansing and crimes against humanity. Another concrete gain is a commitment to double the budget for the Office of the High Commissioner for Human Rights.

Nonetheless, advocates were left lamenting the lack of meaningful, action-oriented agreements on the total package under debate. "Women's groups have been dismayed by a shameful lack of political will on the part of governments to tackle poverty, foster peace and ensure human rights," said a statement issued by a consortium of advocates monitoring the Summit.

Thrown into contention with the late arrival of John Bolton, the controversial presidential pick for US Ambassador to the UN who insisted on hundreds of last-minute amendments and reneged on past commitments, the Summit failed to make any serious commitment to key economic issues and to UN reform—matters of critical importance to women and their families everywhere. The US and a few other wealthy nations refused to commit to a timeframe for increasing official development assistance to 0.7 percent of GNP [gross national product]. (Currently the US gives 0.16 percent, tied for the lowest percentage of GNP with Italy, and gives a paltry 3 cents in aid to Africa of every $100.00 GNP.) Moreover, the US and a handful of allies blocked any meaningful agreement on trade and even watered down further the already weak provisions on climate changes.

Next Steps

In the wake of the World Summit, the main focus of advocacy has now shifted back to the national level where women's groups will continue to push their governments to implement their policy commitments—mapping progress and promoting realistic perspectives on women's day-to-day lives as against the often dry, sterile words of official reports.

Women's groups will continue to press their governments to use sex-disaggragated data to measure and monitor the impact of fiscal and social policies on women compared with men, including those data that have been marginalized or are missing from the MDG. Advocates will also continue to insist that MDG indicators be expanded to include the many gender-sensitive indicators that already exist—including local indicators in national plans drawn up after the Beijing Conference and others developed by international agencies.

At the international level, women's rights advocates will continue to use the MDGS to hold all power players—World Bank and International Monetary Fund, World Trade Organization, the UN and national governments—accountable for creating the necessary enabling conditions for women's empowerment and gender equality. The emphasis thus far has been on what the poorest countries need to do to achieve the goals, the political shift women want to see in the MDGS is more focus on accountability mechanisms that apply to the richest countries, the international financial and trade institutions and transnational corporations, particularly when countries fail to meet the goals due in part to lack of financial resources. Advocates understand that neo-liberal economic policies exacerbate poverty and inequity, contributing to human rights abuses that jeopardize human security. Thus what women really want are their governments to adopt a human rights-based approach to development policy, an approach that puts the well-being of the many above the attainment of mega profits for the very few.

13

The United Nations Should Not Interfere with the Internet

Harold Furchtgott-Roth

Harold Furchtgott-Roth is president of Furchtgott-Roth Economic Enterprises. From 1997 through 2001, he served as commissioner on the Federal Communications Commission (FCC), the federal agency that regulates the communications industry in the United States.

An effort is under way to place the Internet under the control of the United Nations [UN]. Some portray this as a desirable method of reducing U.S. control or influence over the Internet. In reality, the Internet is already free from government interference, to the benefit of users worldwide. The UN's attempt to take control of the Internet is motivated by a desire for greater power and should be stopped.

In Geneva last week, delegates at a U.N. [United Nations] conference recommended that an intergovernmental body should oversee the Internet. At last, according to the European press, pressure from the United Nations and others would result in the American government's loss of control over the Internet.

The only problem is that our government does not actually control the Internet. Still, the United Nations may attempt to seize control of it—the world body's motivation is empire-building.

The Geneva conference was the third preparatory meeting for the U.N. World Summit on the Information Society to be held next month [November 2005] in Tunis. At the Tunis meeting, the United Nations will call for an international body to take over the governance of the Internet. That this resolution will pass is a foregone conclusion. [U.S. ambassador] John Bolton beware.

The U.N. revolution is not about new technologies, but about new empires. The United Nations proposes to take a stateless enterprise, the Internet, and move it under the umbrella of the U.N.

Consumers and businesses around the world have prospered with an Internet that is free of the United Nations.

In December 2003, the United Nations, in typical understatement, issued a proclamation: "We, the representatives of the peoples of the world ... declare our common desire and commitment to build a people-centered, inclusive and development-oriented Information Society ... premised on the purposes and principles of the Charter of the United Nations and respecting fully and upholding the Universal Declaration of Human Rights."

Clamoring for Control

[In June 2005], Secretary-General [Kofi] Annan released the report of the U.N. Working Group on Internet Governance, which, not surprisingly, called for the United Nations to govern the Internet. In September, the European Union followed suit, calling for an intergovernmental body to take over. Now we have last week's calls for international control. The repeated posturing for U.N. control of the Internet is not based on any shortcoming. Rather, the Internet works all too well but is associated with a country that has proven to be unpopular around the world. America is the parent and perhaps even the guardian of the Internet. But it does not govern or control it. For decades, our government funded research and did work on what would eventually become the Internet. Then, rather than exercising a legitimate parentalism, America allowed the Internet to develop free of government guidance or interference.

America could have kept it as a government-only network, excluded other countries or political enemies from using it, taxed or censored it, or monitored every activity imaginable. But it didn't. Americans could have controlled access to the Internet to promote national interests. But we did not.

Our government initially set Internet protocol standards, organized name assignments, and assigned responsibility to third parties for address identifications and look-up procedures for Internet users. In 1998, those responsibilities were transferred to an internationally organized nonprofit group, the Internet Corporation for the Assignment of Names and Numbers [Icann]. Icann has an international board, meets around the world, and does not take instructions from any government. Its bylaws don't even mention the American government. Icann's budget of less than $23 million is lilliputian by U.N. standards.

Today, with the exception of a few totalitarian countries, Internet users don't need to pay any government. Consumers and businesses around the world have prospered with an Internet that is free of the United Nations. Through its proposals next month in Tunis, the world body wants to enrich itself and unwittingly impoverish the Internet. Our challenge is to defend the Internet by keeping it out of the hands of an international bureaucracy.

14

The UN Creates Hysteria by Publishing Misinformation on Climate Change

Marni Soupcoff

Marni Soupcoff is a columnist for the American Enterprise Online *(TAEmag.com).*

Recently three United Nations organizations released a study claiming that climate change was responsible for one-hundred and fifty deaths in 2000. This conclusion is based on an irresponsible use of statistics, drawing conclusions about causalities that are not supported by the evidence. It would be better use of its resources for the United Nations to combat diseases directly instead of drawing questionable conclusions about the weather, leading to actions that will probably not be effective in addressing health issues.

"Global warming kills 150,000 a year," read a dire headline in Britain's *Guardian* on Friday [December 12, 2003], which sounds a bit like an indictment of a particularly active serial killer. But before you go swearing out a warrant for global warming's arrest, keep in mind that frantic predictions of man's doom caused by his poisoning of the world's climate tend not to stand up to a reasoned look at the data. The *Guardian's* hyperbolic headline is no exception.

The *Guardian's* indictment was precipitated by climate talks in Milan [Italy] at which three United Nations [UN] or-

Marni Soupcoff, "Vain Attempts to Change the Weather," *American Enterprise Online*, December 15, 2003. Reproduced with permission of the *American Enterprise*, a national magazine of Politics, Business, and Culture (TAEmag.com).

ganizations—including the World Health Organization—released a study claiming that climate change was directly responsible for 150,000 deaths worldwide in 2000.

A number of objections spring to mind. The most obvious is that, even assuming global warming did cause the deaths (an assumption that will be made by few people save enviroalarmists like [actor] Ed Asner and [former vice president and presidential candidate] Al Gore), this would not warrant the *Guardian's* gloomy conclusion that the statistic is a representative one for every year.

Numbers That Cannot Be Trusted

More importantly, though, the very idea that one can calculate a precise statistic to represent deaths "directly caused" by global warming is ludicrous and irresponsible. Unlike the case of a natural disaster or a plane crash, where it is easy to take toll of those killed or injured, small increases in the earth's temperature do not create obvious and immediate victims whose deaths can be definitively chalked up to warming.

For example, the U.N. report claims that global warming has caused a noticeable increase in malaria and other mosquito-borne diseases. But the report fails to establish convincing proof for a causal connection between climate change and increased incidents of disease, relying instead on the simplistic notion that increases in temperature inevitably lead to more disease.

By assigning an artificial number on the lives lost to global warming, the U.N. is misleadingly implying a scientific certainty and consensus that simply does not exist.

The shortsightedness of this approach has been highlighted by malaria specialist Professor Paul Reiter of the Pasteur Institute and Harvard University, who chides, "it is naive to predict the effects of 'global warming' on malaria on the mere basis of temperature." The history of mosquito-borne diseases is complex, and many factors other than temperature, including agricultural practices and living standards, are often more important in determining the extent of the diseases. How else to explain the fact that malaria was common throughout Europe during the freezing weather of its "Little Ice Age" of the late sixteenth and seventeenth centuries?

Consensus That Does Not Exist

And speaking of ice ages, I'd be remiss not to note that in the midst of the U.N.'s efforts to create hysteria about climate change and drum up support for the Kyoto protocol, a new report in the journal *Climate Change* shows that human-induced global warming may have started as early as 8,000 years ago (so much for blaming hairspray bottles) and might very well have saved the earth from experiencing a new ice age—a fate significantly more perilous to the earth's population than the gradual, three-quarter degree Celsius rise in temperature that scientists predict. (I'm now waiting for the *Guardian* headline about the number of lives saved every year by global warming, but I have a feeling it may be a long wait.)

The bottom line is that by assigning an artificial number on the lives lost to global warming, the U.N. is misleadingly implying a scientific certainty and consensus that simply does not exist. We do not really know if any lives are lost as a direct result of global warming, let alone a quantifiable number.

As Professor Reiter sensibly concludes with respect to the mosquito-borne diseases the U.N. claims are caused by global warming: "Why don't we devote our resources to tackling these diseases directly, instead of spending billions in vain attempts to change the weather?"

The same could rightly be said of all the other health and human rights problems the world faces. It's about time the U.N. and newspapers like the *Guardian* started paying attention to the global problems that really matter. Let's leave the vain attempts to change the weather to the out-of-touch environmental extremists who have nothing better to do with their time.

Organizations to Contact

The editors have compiled the following list of organizations concerned with the issues debated in this book. The descriptions are derived from materials provided by the organizations. All have publications or information available for interested readers. The list was compiled on the date of publication of the present volume; the information provided here may change. Be aware that many organizations take several weeks or longer to respond to inquiries, so allow as much time as possible.

The Better World Campaign (BWC)
1225 Connecticut Ave. NW, 4th Floor, Washington, DC   20036
(202) 462-4900 • fax: (202) 462-2686
Web site: www.betterworldcampaign.org

Founded in 1999, the BWC supports the strengthening of the relationship between the United States and the United Nations through outreach, communications, and advocacy. The BWC Web site includes links to online resources and news articles.

Carnegie Endowment for International Peace
1779 Massachusetts Ave. NW, Washington, DC   20036
(202) 483-7600 • fax: (202) 483-1840
e-mail: Info@CarnegieEndowment.org
Web site: www.carnegieendowment.org

The Carnegie Endowment for International Peace is a private, nonprofit organization dedicated to advancing cooperation between nations and promoting active international engagement by the United States. Its Web site includes links to more than fifty publications addressing some aspect of the work of the United Nations.

Cato Institute

1000 Massachusetts Ave. NW, Washington, DC 20001-5403
(202) 842-0200 • fax (202) 842-3490
Web site: www.cato.org

The Cato Institute, a libertarian public policy foundation
dedicated to promoting limited government, individual liberty, and free markets, believes that the United Nations' lack
of accountability to its member nations has led to corruption
and mismanagement. The institute's numerous publications
include the policy analysis "A Miasma of Corruption: The
United Nations at Fifty."

The Center for UN Reform Education

211 E. 43rd St., Suite 1801, New York, NY 10017
(212) 682-6958 • fax: (212) 682-6959
e-mail: inquiries@centerforunreform.org
Web site: www.centerforunreform.org

The Center for UN Reform Education is an independent,
nonpartisan, nonprofit policy research organization. The mission of the center is to encourage, generate, and sustain discussion of various specific proposals to reform and restructure
the United Nations. Issues addressed include weighted voting
and restructuring of the UN's principal organizations including the Security Council and the General Assembly. In addi-
tion to its Web site, the Center for UN Reform Education
publishes monographs, papers and books, and sponsors edu-
cational events.

The Center for War/Peace Studies (CW/PS)

330 East 38th St., Suite 19Q, New York, NY 10016
(212) 490-6494
Web site: www.cwps.org

The Center for War/Peace Studies, a nonprofit, tax-exempt
U.S. organization, works to establish an international political
and legal system that will make war obsolete. It is developing

the Binding Triad proposal, which would transform the UN General Assembly into a genuine global legislature with the power to enact and enforce laws to promote global peace.

The Heritage Foundation
214 Massachusetts Ave. NE, Washington, DC   20002-4999
(202) 546-4400 • fax: (202) 546-8328
e-mail: info@heritage.org
Web site: www. heritage.org

The Heritage Foundation is a public policy research institute dedicated to the principles of competitive free enterprise, limited government, individual liberty, and a strong national defense. The Heritage Foundation believes that "the tendency of many to rely too heavily on international organizations often creates more problems than it solves." Heritage Foundation publications include "Inside the Asylum: Why the United Nations and Old Europe Are Worse Off than You Think," and "Keep the Internet Free of the United Nations."

The United Nations (UN)
UN Headquarters, New York, NY   10017
e-mail: inquiries2@un.org
Web site: www.un.org

The United Nations offers many publications for a general audience that explain its history, purpose, and activities. The extensive UN Web site includes current news, facts about the UN, and descriptions of UN programs and goals, as well as a live Webcam.

United Nations Foundation
1800 Massachusetts Ave. NW, 4th Floor
Washington, DC   20036
(202) 887-9040 • fax: (202) 887-9021
e-mail: inquiries@un.org
Web site: www.unfoundation.org/about/index.asp

The United Nations Foundation was founded by Ted Turner in 1998 to build and implement public-private partnerships to address the world's most pressing problems. Additional support comes from the Bill and Melinda Gates Foundation. The United Nations Foundation seeks to broaden support for the UN through advocacy, grant writing, and public outreach.

United Nations Institute for Disarmament Research (UNIDIR)

Palais des Nations, Geneva 10   1211
   Switzerland
+41 (0)22 917 3186 • fax: +41 (0)22 917 01 76
e-mail: unidir@unog.ch
Web site: www.unidir.org

The research efforts of UNIDIR are based on the premise that long-term development and economic security are all but impossible in regions torn apart by conflict. As the UNIDIR Web site states, "The global community often invests again and again in the same conflict area, only to have hard-won progress destroyed by the next conflict. Development efforts are wasted unless these conflicts can be tamed and new ones prevented." UNIDIR explores practical measures to bring about disarmament by addressing the root causes of violence.

The United States Institute of Peace (USIP)

1200 Seventeenth St. NW, Washington, DC   20036
(202) 457-1700 • fax: 202 429-6063
Web site: www.usip.org

The United States Institute of Peace is an independent, non-partisan, national institution established and funded by the U.S. Congress. Its task force on the United Nations (UN) assesses the extent to which the United Nations is fulfilling the purposes stated in its charter and makes recommendations to the U.S. government on UN-related policy decisions.

Women's International League for Peace and Freedom (WILPF)

1, rue de Varembe, Case Postale 28, Geneva 20   1211
   Switzerland

e-mail: inforequest@wilpf.ch
Web site: www.wilpf.int.ch/index.htm

The WILPF, founded in 1915, is the oldest women's peace organization in the world. It has maintained consultative relations with the United Nations (UN) since 1948. WILPF works for democratization of the UN, including the Security Council, monitors activities of the Security Council to promote reform, and opposes what it views as the privatization and corporatization of the UN. The WILPF would like to abolish the Security Council veto.

World Federalist Movement Institute for Global Policy
708 Third Ave., 24th Floor, New York, NY   10017
(212) 599 1320 • fax: (212) 599-1332
e-mail: info@wfm.org
Web site: www.wfm.org/site/index.php/base/main

The World Federalist Movement supports the creation of democratic global structures accountable to the citizens of the world. Its publications include "The Case for a United Nations Parliamentary Assembly," and "The International Criminal Court," volumes 1 and 2.

World Food Programme (WFP)
Via C.G.Viola 68, Parco dei Medici 00148, Rome
   Italy
e-mail: wfpinfo@wfp.org
Web site: www.wfp.org/english

The World Food Programme is the food aid agency of the United Nations. It carries out targeted interventions aimed at providing emergency food aid to refugees, improving the nutrition for economically disadvantaged persons, and building assets to promote self-reliance and end poverty.

Bibliography

Books

Madeleine Korbel Albright
Madam Secretary. New York: Miramax Books, 2003.

Kofi A. Annan
"We the Peoples . . .": Nobel Peace Message. New York: Ruder Finn Press, 2002.

Jed L. Babbin
Inside the Asylum: Why the U.N. and Old Europe Are Worse than You Think. Washington, DC: Regnery Publishing, 2004.

Michael N. Barnett
Eyewitness to a Genocide: The United Nations and Rwanda. Ithaca, NY: Cornell University Press, 2002.

David Carment and Albrecht Schnabel
Conflict Prevention: Path to Peace or Grand Illusion? New York: United Nations University Press, 2003.

Romeo Dallaire
Shake Hands with the Devil: The Failure of Humanity in Rwanda. New York: Carroll & Graf, 2005.

Linda M. Fasulo
An Insider's Guide to the UN. New Haven, CT: Yale University Press, 2003.

Mary Ann Glendon
A World Made New: Eleanor Roosevelt and the Universal Declaration of Human Rights. New York: Random House, 2001.

Dore Gold   *Tower of Babble: How the United Na-
                         tions Has Fueled Global Chaos.* New
                         York: Crown Forum, 2004.

Robert F. Gorman *Great Debates at the United Nations:
                         An Encyclopedia of Fifty Key Issues
                         1945–2001.* Westport, CT: Green-
                         wood, 2001.

Paul M. Kennedy   *The Parliament of Man: The Past,
                         Present, and Future of the United Na-
                         tions.* New York: Random House,
                         2006.

Sadako N. Ogata   *The Turbulent Decade: Confronting
                         the Refugee Crises of the 1990s.* New
                         York: W.W. Norton, 2005.

Edmund Jan   *Encyclopedia of the United Nations
Osmanczyk   and International Agreements.* New
                         York: Routledge, 2003.

David Rieff   *At the Point of a Gun: Democratic
                         Dreams and Armed Intervention.* New
                         York: Simon & Schuster, 2005.

Scott Ritter   *Iraq Confidential: The Untold Story of
                         the Intelligence Conspiracy to Under-
                         mine the UN and Overthrow Saddam
                         Hussein.* New York: Nation Books,
                         2005.

Pedro A. Sanjuan *The UN Gang: A Memoir of Incompe-
                         tence, Corruption, Espionage, Anti-
                         Semitism, and Extremism at the UN
                         Secretariat.* New York: Doubleday,
                         2005.

Stephen C.
Schlesinger
Act of Creation: The Founding of the United Nations: A Story of Superpowers, Secret Agents, Wartime Allies and Enemies, and Their Quest for a Peaceful World. Boulder: Westview, 2003.

The Stanley
Foundation
Capturing the 21st Century Security Agenda: Prospects for Collective Responses. Muscatine, IA: The Stanley Foundation 2004.

Martin Stanton
Somalia on Five Dollars a Day: A Soldier's Story. Novato, CA: Presidio, 2001.

Chris E. Stout
Psychology of Terrorism: Coping with the Continued Threat. Westport, CT: Praeger, 2004.

Sandrine Tesner
The United Nations and Business: A Partnership Recovered. New York: St. Martin's, 2000.

Periodicals

America
"Failure of Leadership," October 3, 2005.

Kofi Annan
"How Can We Adapt to Climate Change?" *China Daily*, November 9, 2006.

Amir Attaran
"Necessary Measures," *New York Times*, September 13, 2005.

Elizabeth Becker
"UN Official Plans to Urge U.S. to Reconsider Its Food Policies," *New York Times*, September 24, 2003.

Catholic Insight   "UN Continues to Push Abortion,"
                        February 2005.

Blanche Wiesen   "Eleanor Roosevelt's Human Rights
Cook   Legacy," *Peace and Freedom*, Spring
                        2006.

Ivo H. Daalder   "Pushing the UN to Act When It
and James M.   Must," *Boston Globe*, December 4,
Lindsay   2004.

Economist   "Time for a Re-Think: The United
                        Nations," November 20, 2004.

Paul Johnson   "The UN Is for Talk, Not Action,"
                        Forbes, March 14, 2005.

Debayani Kar   "Missing the Kairos Moment? The
                        U.N. World Summit Comes Up
                        Short," *Sojourners*, December 2005.

Jeane Kirkpatrick   "UN Human Rights Panel Needs
                        Some Entry Standards," *International
                        Herald Tribune*, May 14, 2003.

Tony Mauro   "Be Wary of Internet 'Governance,'"
                        USA Today, November 16, 2005.

Gideon Rachman   "Change in America Will Not Solve
                        the United Nations' Crisis," *The Fi-
                        nancial Times*, November 14, 2006.

Tina Rosenberg   "A Video Game That Teaches Battling
                        Hunger, Not People," *New York Times
                        Upfront*, January 30, 2006.

Daniel B. Schneider	"A Love-Hate Affair: The United Nations and the United States Have Long Been Ambivalent About Each Other. But as the UN Marks Its 60th Anniversary, the Relationship Is More Complicated than Ever," *New York Times Upfront*, September 19, 2005.
Seattle Post-Intelligencer	"United Nations Essential to World Peace and Security," August 15, 2006.
Silvano M. Tomasi	"United Nations Reform and Human Rights," *America*, September 12, 2005.
Fareed Zakaria	"When the U.N. Fails, We All Do," *Newsweek*, December 13, 2004.

Index